STEPPES TO FLEET STREET

STEPPES TO FLEET STREET

by

OLGA FRANKLIN

LONDON
VICTOR GOLLANCZ LTD
1968

First published March 1968
Second impression March 1968
Third impression July 1968

575 00023 6

Printed in Great Britain by
The Camelot Press Ltd., London and Southampton

For Beryl

CONTENTS

CONTENTS

CHAPTER I

EXODUS

FATHER WAS THE kind of man who never stopped talking about his relations.

One day he would put them all in a book and that, he said, would pay them back for all the times they had refused when he wanted to borrow some money.

He complained that all his relations were ridiculous, particularly his Mother. One thing he disliked about her was that she was Russian. This greatly annoyed my Father, who admired the English and wanted very much to pass as one of them.

One of his favourite stories about Grandmother was that she had been raped as a young girl by soldiers of the Czar's army. She always denied it. She said her third son Izzy never liked her, and was always trying to blacken her character. The truth was that she had only looked at the soldiers sleeping in the next room. Her Father had bolted her in her own room for a week while the soldiers were billeted on his farm at Utyena in the province of Kovno. She made a peephole in the wall and that was all. Later she told the whole farm what she had seen and heard, and mentioned that the soldiers were all goodlooking, so this cost her her reputation in that village.

We six children, brought up in a respectable Birmingham suburb, always had Grandma for breakfast, and though our Mother was not against it, because she didn't like Grandma either, she worried about the effect on us.

"Do you have to tell such things in front of the children?" our Mother always said.

One half of the family was born in Russia and the other half on various voyages back and forth between Riga and Grimsby. Grandmother took an instant dislike to England on her first trip, and insisted on sailing right home again as soon as Grandfather could find the fare. You had to have £1 to land in England, as my family did on the first occasion in 1874. Those who had no pound were sent back to Russia, along with anyone considered unfit through snow-blindness or other defect. The journey from Riga, where Grandfather, wife and four children embarked, cost £2, and if you could pay another £2 on top you could sail on to America. Most of the immigrants, simple village folk like my own family, the Izvozchiks, who couldn't read or write, thought Grimsby was America anyway. Grandfather was a poor glazier from Minsk in White Russia who was brought up in a " molitv-yenny dom", a prayer-house.

The pick of Grandma's trousseau, that is, forty pairs of woollen stockings, were stolen that first day they found lodging in a house in Nelson Street. That did it. Grandma wanted to go home. She would sit down and write to her Father in Utyena and tell him to send the horses to Riga to meet the return boat. Only the problem was that she couldn't write, and the last pound had gone on getting permission to land.

Although she had another six children by her husband, it was the end of their marriage in one sense. Grandmother couldn't forgive the poor man for bringing her to England.

To get away from her complaints and moans about the stolen stockings, the little man from Minsk named Leib Izvozchik went down to the docks close by to see about getting some food for the family. When a boat arrived with a good catch of fresh cod, he helped to carry the nets and baskets between the slippery decks and the shore, and in exchange was given a large cod, still leaping about in its basket. It was hard work, Father said, getting that cod to lie still long enough to be cooked for their first supper. The fish kept leaping off the table, and had to be brought back by the eldest children.

It took nearly five years for Grandfather to scratch together enough money for Grandmother and the children to go home to her Father. It was decided that Leib should stay behind and try to make his fortune on his own, and then return to Russia with it in a few years' time, with the object of making a good impression on his father-in-law and persuading him to let Leib have a share in the farm and horse-dealing business.

It all ended badly, and the family, now destitute, returned to England for a second time. But my Father had never got over it. Grandma, in his opinion, was potty. Her old home, which she never stopped boasting about because it had fourteen windows, was only a big wooden hut; the thatched roof was full of mice; there were wolves outside and so much snow that you couldn't open the door in winter.

Father said the whole story was fit really just for the comic papers.

Listening to him, we had to laugh obediently at potty old Russian Grandma who hadn't been on speaking terms with us anyway. Though, to me, the real joke was that no one was more Russian than my Father, with his fair hair and blue eyes and the way he liked to annoy our Mother by singing and dancing for us at the breakfast table, while still in his pyjamas and the top half all unbuttoned.

At least, looking back he made it sound just comic. How Grandma beat all her five sons for fighting, using a stick or umbrella or anything that came to hand. The older ones were beaten for hitting the younger ones, and the younger ones for crying when they were hit.

I was given the name Olga because of Grandma. Some people think that names don't matter, but I think they do. It marked me out from the others who all had nice English or other names. They were called Beryl, Cora, Bettina, Felix and George. I was the only one to be beaten for being wild and rough. And yet I was also expected to *be* wild and rough because I was an Olga.

Father would approach the breakfast table like a vaudeville star ready to take his audience by storm. He had a special taste for heartbreaking verse or rhyme.

> "Prop your eyes wide open, Joey,
> For I've brought you something great.
> Apples, no—a deal sight better . . ."

This recitation ended with the tragic death of Joey, the little cripple boy, and most of us in tears, until Mother would remark that, though Grandma might be potty, her least favourite son was even worse.

"Your Father's family were all horse-thieves and had no manners at all," said Mother who had been a Manchester hospital nurse before marriage. To which Father replied: "Horse stealing was a highly skilled trade, there was a lot of competition."

"You see," said Mother while rapping my brother's knuckles with a spoon for eating with his knife, "just ruffians. No wonder my children put knives in their mouths."

"One day," Father said, "Olyechka will put them all in a book." That was his name for me on my good days.

Anything started him off on a new instalment of that ill-fated flight home to Russia, which ended with them all crying in the snow, and a mad uncle making rude faces at them through each one of those fourteen windows in turn.

If Mother only sewed a button on to George's shirt, it reminded him. Auntie Rosie, as a child, sewed shirts to feed the whole family.

"Stitch, stitch, stitch, in poverty, hunger and dirt," Father sang to us between mouthfuls of porridge, "and still in a voice of dolorous pitch, she sang the song of the shirt."

"Your Auntie Rose was the only good one," Father said. "She was only a tiny little girl, but she had a good singing voice. And so, when we all got back to Grimsby, Rosie sang in the streets to get money for us."

Mother said we should all eat up our dinner and go back to school, but Father had noticed that the boys had left their greens on their plates. "Oh, sharper than a serpent's tooth," shouted Father, "is the ungrateful child."

He was keen on theatres and music-halls, and knew by heart whole plays or entire sets of verses from them.

Father said that Izvozchik family could have lived for a week all eleven of them, on what my twin brothers left on their plates. Felix and George, pale as death, got ready to run. They firmly believed that if the Russian relations were mad as hatters, which seemed extremely likely, then our Father was the maddest of the lot. They couldn't stand being in the same room with him.

Father was romantic, too. He became emotional telling us about Oliver Twist, for he saw himself as Oliver. So I think it upset him to realise that his own real name had been plain Izzy Izvozchik, and not the distinguished-sounding Henry Davis, as he called himself. Izvozchik was an awful name even in Russia, where it really meant a "coachman". It was more a term of abuse than a name.

On the second arrival in England, in the autumn of 1880, the family managed to get as far as Birmingham, where Grandfather took the eldest boys Dave and Abe to the Jews' Free School.

"Moy starshy sin Davvid" (my eldest son David) said Grand-father, pushing the eldest one forward.

"Ah, Davis!" said the Headmaster thankfully, "that's a nice name."

So the Izvozchiks became the Davises, though, as no one could read or write English, no one outside the school knew how to spell it.

Later on some of the Izvozchik children were registered as
Davies and some as Davis, but no one seemed to mind. And that's
why none of our family had birth certificates which matched. As
Grandma went on giving birth, it was left to the Registrar to spell
our name whichever way he fancied. But we were marked out
just the same, in a special way. "They called us," said Father, "the
Poor Davises. Nobody liked us."

I do think perhaps he was a bit hard on Grandma. It must have
been difficult to adjust to being a mother of nine children in a
Birmingham back-to-back slum after being a spoiled little rich
girl in Russia. It wasn't easy bringing up all those children. As a
grown girl she never even had to dress herself. She didn't know
how to sew, and most of the children's clothing came from the
"charity".

Later on when her favourite son Abe was earning enough to
keep them all, as well as an extra penny a week for a weekly bath,
she had an Irish servant called Sarah. But Sarah couldn't be trusted
to beat the boys as hard as she did, when they tried running off to
school or selling papers without first saying their hour-long prayers.

Every night she climbed the narrow staircase to the room above
to stop the fighting.

"Who threw Mo out of bed?" Dave and Abe and Izzy pretended to be asleep, while young Mo howled on the bare floor.

What embittered Grandma was that her husband could not be
trusted with the beating either. He behaved as though he were
scared of his own sons.

They liked him Father said. He wasn't potty like Grandma.
Leib Izvozchik realised that it was worth all the hardship and
having no servants, just to be in England. Especially as a few
months later Czar Alexander II was assassinated, and the pogroms
and all the raping and troubles began.

Father told us his story, as I said, over and over. And never once
said a good word for Grandma.

CHAPTER II

FROM MOTHER RUSSIA

UTYENA TODAY IS a thriving little country town with its own ancient market. Here they raise hogs and sheep, grow and make flax and textiles, honey and beeswax. There are now even a few small machine-tool factories, making tools to be sent to other parts of the Soviet Union.

There was a hamlet in Utyena even in the tenth century. A fortified castle stood on one of the many hills sweeping upwards from the muddy banks of the River Nieman. It was always being attacked by the Teutons from the thirteenth century onwards. Even today the Soviet Russian tourists who come this way like to point out the beautiful white columns of the former bourgeois landlord's mansion, standing among pine forests well away from the old village.

Some of the richer peasants had homes with tiled roofs, and these houses were always guarded by savage dogs. Most of the cottages had thatched roofs standing in tiny patches of land, some no bigger than an English back garden.

Our Babushka (Grandmother) lived with her parents and one brother in the second largest house just outside the village. It had only a thatched roof, but it stood well away from the poor Jews' hovels, which were sometimes no more than tiny log cabins black with age, some of them quite lopsided as they sank with each year deeper and deeper into the sand. Inside these hovels was darkness lit only by an unprotected oil lamp. It was here, all along the road from Kovno to Jurburg, half buried in sand in summer and snow in winter, that the poor Jews lived. Our great-grandfather Berl Yofa was a Russian who had come from Kiev many years ago, which is a polite way of saying that under Czar Alexander II and a whole lot of new laws called "Akty Yuzhnoi i Zapadnoy Rossii" (Laws for South and West Russia) his family were told to go and live in the Kovno valley instead.

However, he spoke Russian, which meant that he was able to run a business, to attend Court when necessary for the paying or collecting of taxes, and by paying bribes to keep on the right side of the authorities who, by law, were forbidden to use any other language but Russian in order to assimilate everybody into the Czar's empire.

In this way Berl was able to acquire a large piece of land, to employ servants, to build farm dwellings and stables and to start business with the money previously accumulated from the selling and leasing of liquor. He traded in the breeding, sale and export of Zmuda horses. These are small but exceptionally strong horses widely used in the surrounding countryside, where horses were needed to pull the plough in muddy, swampy valley fields.

The hovels and the better-off homes were separated by ancient lime trees. The view was splendid, overlooking pine forests and lakes. This part of the country used to be famous for its honey from millions of bees nesting in the holes of lime tree trunks, producing some of the finest honey in the world.

This was the country of thousands of lakes so large that they ran into one another, cascading into rapids and waterfalls. Through and among them ran the River Nieman.

In the decades following the Crimean war, cholera broke out over Russia every summer. Soon the rich farmer Berl Yofa (or Jaffe or Jofa, as some spelled it) was beating his breast in orthodox manner with those soft, white hands of his, as one child after another died in the plague. Twelve of his children died. Once there were fourteen children, one for each of the proud house's fourteen windows. Then there were only two children left. One

was our Grandmother and the other a silly son, Yasha, considered
to be no better than the village idiot.

She was spoilt. It was the custom for rich Russian merchants
to pamper their daughters. They were waited on by nannies and
housemaids and servants all their lives. And it was, and always
has been, the habit of Jews who could afford it to copy what their
Gentile neighbours did. She had weak eyes. So not even a tutor
was allowed to come to the house. She was not allowed to learn
to sew or embroider. So she did nothing, just sat. Her ignorance
of the outside world was total.

The only excitement in this stifling life was the weekly market
in summer when merchants and gypsies, sometimes with caravans
of circus entertainers and clowns and performing bears and a
ragged Jewish orchestra, arrived in the market-place with their
stalls and carpets and linens, their pots of honey and medicines,
their vats of salt herring and oil, their strings of onions. On these
days Grandma, in her finery and her frizzy blond plaits, sat
blinking her small blue eyes in the sunshine and watching the
busy scene like a village queen, certain of her position as the rich
horse-dealer's only daughter.

The old man Berl Yofa did not want her to marry. She was all
he had. His wife bored him. He blamed her for the one surviving
stupid son and for the deaths of the other children.

The village matchmaker called at least twice a year, bringing
a set of photographs and brief biographies of eligible suitors.
Photography was popular even in those remote rural districts, and
it was the fashion for whole families to be photographed at the
weekly market, or travelling artists were invited to make a
drawing, sometimes in colour.

One day Berl agreed to look. What attracted him was the fact
that the young suitor from Minsk, Leib Izvozchik, was an orphan,
willing to come and live on the farm in Utyena.

It was winter. The best way, normally, would be to go to

Minsk by the River Nieman, which took passenger traffic in little vessels, sometimes pulled by 100 men or floated downstream with sails. To come back upstream they were towed by men or punted with long poles.

This traffic had begun with the Crimean war, when the British, French and Turks blockaded many of the Russian seaports and the Nieman (or Nemunas or Neman) became an important water-way for merchandise and traffic.

For the four winter months the river was frozen. Berl, having made up his mind, was anxious to get the whole business over.

They set out by sledge, drawn by his own small horses no bigger than ponies, for the three-day journey. Their destination was one of the scores of Jewish inns on the highroad. This was to be their halfway house for a meeting with the suitor and his sponsoring party, who had already agreed to travel northwards from White Russia and meet the Yofa party on the border.

If all the wolves and bears and lynx that Father said came out of the pine forests to attack the little marriage party in their sledge actually did so, then I doubt if the wedding would ever have been celebrated. Besides, a great number of bears and lynx had been wiped out by poachers and hunting parties of the Grand Dukes of all the Russias, who liked spending their holidays in these parts. But elks, deer and wild goats did roam the forests, and sprang across the path of travellers.

It was the first long journey Grandma had ever made.

In spite of the wild goats roaming around looking for food, in spite of tipping the sledge over into lakes and streams and even into ponds of foaming rapids, the party safely arrived and were given rooms at the inn.

It was 1868. Anton Chekhov, many miles south in Taganrog, was in his first year at grammar school. In his stories he has described many of these Jewish inns of the period. The dark, stifling rooms, the smells of cooking, the countless children popping up from piles of rugs and clothing and mysterious divans and grinning at him like so many Cheshire cats, the ragged, overworked servants. Above all Anton Pavlovitch always remembered the kindly, stout Jewish woman innkeeper who took him in half-dead and nursed him when, as a fourteen-year-old schoolboy, he caught a fever from bathing on a summer holiday.

And so, because Chekhov has made it so real, this was always, for me, the best part of Father's story.

Leib Izvozchik, calling himself Levi ben David, was only twenty-two, that is, two years younger than the bride-to-be. And it was no surprise to find that apart from his sponsor, from the "molitvyenny dom", the prayer-house at Minsk (which had at that time nine such schools or Yeshivas all carefully listed in the Czar's police gazette and lawbooks), Leib had also brought his mother. It was the practice among both Russians and Jews to call a child an orphan if he had no father. Mothers just did not count, especially if they had no money to educate their children.

The whole of the first day at the inn was spent in an examination of the qualifications of Leib. He was tested in Torah (the law), in his knowledge of Talmudic learning, and so on. He had to recite for some hours all the necessary hymns and prayers for every possible occasion. He had been taught Hebrew, Russian and arithmetic, the two latter subjects being taught compulsorily in accordance with the laws introduced by Czar Alexander II. Boys who studied Russian with the object of teaching it to others were automatically freed from the obligation of military service. Later the new Czar Nicholas II changed all that.

After that the Chozyaika (woman innkeeper) placed a white cloth on the table, and set out the prikuski (hors d'œuvres) of herring and sour cream, with black bread and tea. The tea was served with jam if there was no lemon, or with a lump of sugar held and sucked in the mouth while the glass of tea was drunk.

The difficulty was to fix a date for the wedding. Berl was often away from home, travelling with his caravan of horses and men to all the frontiers, including the port of Riga, to ship his horses abroad. So why not have the wedding here and now? The match-maker was given his commission. The sponsor from Minsk was given his expenses and donation to the boys of his school. Some of the lace and linen brought along as exhibits from Utyena to be shown to the bridegroom as part of the marriage settlement were unpacked and shown to the gushing innkeeper's wife who, with cries of joy at all this unexpected business, rushed off to the kitchen to prepare a feast. A wedding canopy was improvised with a shabby rug from the innkeeper's floor. In no time at all a half-starved Jewish fiddler was produced, and in the next three days the marriage was solemnised and the Poor Davises were launched at last.

Or rather, they were very nearly so. The couple were allowed —when standing under the canopy—a glance at each other's face. But no more. It just was not possible in that country inn, miles from any town, to organise a "mikvah" a ritual bath for brides, at a moment's notice. They just had to wait until they all got home three days and three nights later to Utyena. No bath, no bed, said our Father in disgust. That's Jews for you.

Father didn't care for Jews any more than he did for Russians. In fact he didn't really like foreigners at all, except for making sport of their funny ways. He said pious Jews were terrible hypo-crites because they were always "schnorrering", that is, going round with the collection box for money for the poor. Father said it was quite different for him to go to his brothers Abe and Mo and try to borrow money, because that wasn't for the poor but for us.

After the wedding the bridegroom just went on as before, saying his prayers most of the day. Only now he had two small boys to teach to pray as well. Also he had collected some tools for mending windows. He was going to learn a trade, and then

they could all emigrate to England or America. It was odd that
the old man didn't try to stop them leaving. It was even odder
that Berl didn't realise that it was silly to let his spoiled and helpless daughter and his unsophisticated son-in-law go out into the
world alone and unprotected.

They set off one spring morning in the open cart with the hood
down as it was fine. They needed four horses to drag the load to
Kovno station. In front sat the coachman and the courier who was
to see them across the frontier, pay the Customs dues and see that
they caught the right boat. In the cart itself there was hardly room
for the two of them with the four oldest children.

On to the cart the servants piled everything they would need
to set up home abroad. An oil stove, a samovar, bedding, mat-
tresses, chairs, furniture, some rugs and cloths, a mirror, a side-
board, linen, the children's toys and clothes, supplies of tea and
flour and sugar, all the children's prayer and hymn books, and, of
course, Grandma's forty pairs of stockings.

Grandma had noticed the other much poorer immigrants go
past her house sometimes, Lithuanian peasants were leaving home
by the thousand every year. They were deserting the dust bowls
and sandpits created by earlier generations, including many
Jewish merchants, who had torn up the forests and made fortunes
from their timber. Now the peasants were starving on their
barren earth, living by poaching from the lakes and forests. Every
day they trailed by on the high road to Riga, with their hand-
carts and their bundles, en route for Grimsby, Liverpool and New
York. They took only what they could carry. Grandmother, in
her inexperience, thought it was all they possessed, and perhaps it
was.

So now, nearly seven years after the marriage in the inn on the
road to Minsk, the Izvozchiks were on their way for two sover-
eigns, for the rough week-long crossing of the Baltic and then the
North Sea, with everything, including the kitchen stove.

It was lucky, therefore, that they were robbed of nearly every piece of property at successive stopping points along the way to Riga. When they finally climbed on to the boat for England, they had with them only those pieces which they and the children could carry. Some bedding and Grandma's forty pairs of stockings were all that was left.

That little ship, a 1,000-ton passenger vessel, owned by the Great Central Railway Company who also owned the docks of Grimsby, Lincolnshire, England, had few comforts to offer. It was the second unpleasant surprise for the Izvozchiks, after the loss of all their household goods. They had seen pictures and drawings of the new, great, ocean-going liners which plied between Riga and Hamburg and Grimsby and Liverpool and America. They were nothing like this. The foredeck of the steamer was crowded with ragged immigrants, whose only shelter was the bridge deck above or the shadow of the fo'c'sle.

However, stewards brought hot drinks, and sometimes bowls of hot potatoes were handed round. Some of the immigrants looked half-starved already; they lay on rags, clutching hunks of black bread and sugar in a ball, biting at each in turn. The sugar, it was believed, kept some sort of body heat which helped them to face the medical examination on landing, before an Immigration Board presided over by the Stipendiary Magistrate.

The trouble was that ships used for this cheap immigrant traffic were chartered by the railway companies to private owners. The ships were often old, and not always seaworthy. Sometimes fires broke out, and sometimes immigrants were lost at sea from these small ships which were barely 300-feet, 1,000-ton vessels. They had to be small anyway, in order to get through the Grimsby lockpits and come straight through, swing round and berth just inside, anchoring within 100 yards of the hostel where penniless immigrants slept.

From 1860 until 1900, and then on a smaller scale up to the

outbreak of the First World War, this traffic made a lot of money for the private shipping companies.

Grandma, of course, queening it as usual and not understanding that she was no longer to be treated as the rich horse-dealer's daughter but only as a poor immigrant seeking shelter, didn't fancy staying the night in the Grimsby hostel with its deal tables each decorated with an aspidistra and its wooden benches for diners, with simple bedding laid on the floor. Instead she marched straight into 117, Nelson Street, which was quite a nice house, and sat down, expecting as usual to be waited on.

It was not what Leib had led her to expect. The house in Nelson Street looked imposing enough, nearly as good as the fine buildings in Kovno, but it was packed with people. The Izvozchik family were given one room for the seven of them, including the baby. The other passengers who disembarked more sensibly went straight to the Grimsby hostel, only a few yards from both the boat and the train which would next day take them on to Liverpool and America or simply to Manchester, or to the East End of London.

A Rabbi met every boat to help the Jews on board. Daphne Genlis, who lives in Grimsby, told me that her Grandfather was one of them.

"There was no charitable committee at that time, and no synagogue. Grandfather went down to the docks every time a ship came in, and helped in whatever ways he could. He was an extremely poor man, and often my Grandmother would be in despair over his generosity to these people. He used to go round the community asking for their support as well. The people who settled in Grimsby were those with no money to go further."

And that included the Izvozchiks, who were penniless very quickly. By the time they'd been turned out of prosperous, respectable Nelson Street, it was too late to register at the Grimsby hostel. The hostel had once been a railway-station, and looked it.

The dining-room, for example, had one wall roughly bricked in where the railway tunnel had been.

They spent the rest of the summer in Grimsby, sleeping rough, with occasional begging and living on bits of cod thrown to them from the fishing-boats.

When at last they were given a pound and told to move on, it was the obvious thing to make for Birmingham, where some poor families from Utyena were already settled.

It wasn't nice for Grandma, in the year that followed, having to call on these former neighbours of hers, whom she had once despised for their miserable poverty with hardly a patch of soil to grow a cabbage upon. Cabbage made a nourishing bortsch, even when you had no meat to put in it, and whole families could live on them alone.

Grandpa's earnings from the window-mending were never more than a few pennies a time. And now there were Dave and Abe and Phoebe and Rose as well as Izzy and Mo and Becky, and soon Sam and Sally, to feed. If it hadn't been for her favourite boy Abie, whose earnings selling matches and papers on the streets kept the whole family, they would all have starved. Clever Abie bought scraps of rag and cloth and cheap rugs from street markets. Grandma stuffed them in a sack, put it on her back and went to call on her former neighbours from Utyena, now living respectably in Varna Road and Handsworth and back of Broad Street among the real Black Country immigrants from Halesowen, Tamworth and Walsall.

Grandma had only one ambition now. To scrape together every penny, every shilling that Abe and the other children could earn. It took very nearly five years to find the £2 for the fare home.

It was November 1879. She was pregnant again. A letter came from her Father saying that he was ill, and she decided not to wait any longer.

Her impulsive return home was even madder than her first

exodus. Many of the northern seaports would already be frozen. The Nieman would be frozen too, and the main highway to Kovno would be packed high with snow. But the railway would be running, at least from Riga to Kovno. And her Father would send the courier and horses to meet them, when they got Abie's letter.

This time they had almost the whole of the steerage deck to themselves.

When people think of Russian Jews, if they ever do, they tend to think of a lot of bearded chaps in peaked caps of the style affected today by modish boys and shawled women in sheitels (wigs), all emigrating from the old country with accents like Peter Ustinov's when he's being funny on television. In fact, the truth is quite otherwise. They were all different and, like the Izvozchiks, not usually on speaking terms, one tribe with another.

There were the educated ones from Moscow, Leningrad, Kiev, Kharkov, and so on, who didn't know a word of Yiddish or Hebrew, who all won gold medals at their local gymnasium or grammar school entitling them to a university career. Then there were the uneducated ones with no gold medals who lived inside Czarist Russia illegally—instead of outside in the Pale of Settlement where they were supposed to live. They were Russian-speaking but had no grammar, and many of these, after being pushed about by the police and denounced by informers who could earn a few roubles by Jew-spotting, left for the United States. You will find many of them in Hollywood and similar places, and a large number serve in the New York police force and nearly died with excitement when Nikita Krushchev went to New York in 1959. As I found when I got caught there in the crush.

It all depended on which year you emigrated, and with whom. And it is worth recounting here because the histories of such emigrations are few and far between. And the only reason why the Izvozchik history was handed down to me was, quite simply, that Grandma was a snob. She couldn't bear the idea of being mixed up with those poor, starving Lithuanians, Russians and Jewish revolutionaries who got beaten up in pogroms and their wooden homes set alight while they were forced to flee shouting "a weh a weh!". And now Grandma was full of weh (woe) too, but not because of pogroms but because she felt she'd been let down by fast-talking Grandpa who'd painted to her this glowing picture of wonderful England with fine ladies and gentlemen riding about in droshkys, where any poor Jew who didn't rightly know a Nominative case from a Genitive one could become a full English citizen with rights.

Well, she'd seen now what it was like. A slum house first of all in Inge Street and then in Singer's Hill, Holloway Head, Birmingham, with just two bare rooms, one up one down, and nothing to eat. And no money, except what the children earned. Now they were going home; and she hoped she need never see England again.

When the family arrived back at Riga, there were no horses waiting to take them home to Utyena. There was no courier, no message, nothing.

There was nothing for it but to sell some of the children's clothing to pay for the railway fare to Kovno. Izzy's good boots, which had been a present from a charitable committee in Birmingham, had to be sacrificed. So he was the one allowed to put his feet on the iron box inside the third class railway carriage with its hard wooden benches for seats. The iron box was filled with hot water or sometimes some chemical to heat the carriage. It was stone cold, though, long before they reached Kovno. Yet the the children quite enjoyed the journey, running through the corridor, shouting in English, which Abe and Phoebe could now speak fluently.

Arriving at Kovno, they all ran excitedly along the platform, looking for some of the servants who always came to meet the trains. But there was no one there. No men and no horses.

They started to walk through the snow until they were picked up by neighbours with a cart and four horses. My Father's feet in their old felt slippers, which were wrapped around and stuck together with cardboard, were hurting.

The neighbours said it was a good thing she had come home at last, for the old man had been very ill and was now either dead or dying.

It was the climax of Father's story. He used to get up from his chair and walk up and down our big kitchen, telling it. He would stop at this point, to remind me that it ought to go in a book. He said that when Dickens had been writing *The Old Curiosity Shop* in instalments and it was clear that Little Nell was going to die, people were so upset that they wrote to him and begged that she should be saved. But, of course, Nell had to die, Father said. Because it was the story that mattered. It had to be a true-to-life story and no one could stop that. He said that, even when you saw the end in the beginning, there was nothing you could do to stop it.

When they got to the farm, it was still light. She didn't let the children run; they picked up their bundles and stumbled over the white stiff fields and past the stables and into the yard, which made the dogs start barking furiously.

When no one came to open the door, they started to run the length of the house trying to look through some of the fourteen windows of the low, one-storey house.

Then, suddenly, she saw her half-mad brother Yasha grimacing at her from one window. When she rushed towards him, he darted away and made faces at the next. Then the next after that. It went on, like some grotesque game of hide-and-seek.

Then there was a great clanking of chains and the door, to her great relief, was unbolted. In it stood a Russian peasant woman of perhaps nearly forty years of age. Grandma thought she recognised one of the women who used to work for her Father on the farm.

"Go away," said the woman in Russian. "I am the mistress here now. I married your brother a few days ago. Your Father is dead and Yasha is master here. You are not wanted."

Then she chained and bolted the door again.

They stayed in Utyena throughout the winter, spring, summer and autumn, trying to get help from friends and relatives. They advised her to find an "advokat", a solicitor, and to sue in the courts of Kovno for her rightful share of her Father's inheritance. There was a large sum of money as well as the farm and property, and she had a special right to it, in view of the fact that her brother was not, and never had been, a responsible, normal person.

So they stayed on, and there were long talks with this lawyer and with that one. Some advised her to go to law; some said it would cost too much. Anyway, where was the money to come from for the lawsuit?

In the end, there was nothing for it but to go back to Grimsby even if they died of hunger before they got there. She wrote to Leib to come to Grimsby to meet them and to bring some money if possible. I never could understand why Father didn't admire her as I did. For her courage at least.

The voyage back was, as she called it, "ujass", terrible. And Father never forgave her for that useless journey.

The Poor Davises were never able to forgive anybody anything. That was their trouble.

CHAPTER III

BRUM

IT HAS ALL gone now; their Victorian world of the Bull Ring and the Fish Market and my old school in New Street dating back to Elizabethan times, founded by King Edward VI.

It has all gone now; the narrow streets of black houses between Jamaica Row and Holloway Head where Grandfather Izvozchik used to go with plates of glass on his back, looking for windows to mend; where the good son Abe started work at thirteen learning upholstery at Gordon's furnishers for 2/6 a week, including one penny for the weekly bath.

It has all gone now; the yellow trams taking the children to the Lickey Hills to pick bilberries; iced buns from the baker in Bristol Street; barefoot boys outside the greengrocer shops, which smelled of oranges and nuts and chestnuts and wet holly.

And the ghetto has gone too, where the Poor Davises grew up. But in those days it was not too far from the slums into the fields. Grandfather pushed a little hand-cart up the Hagley Road, and there beyond Bearwood was the open country, where he and the children Sam and Sally picked laurels and the red rose-hips to take home and decorate the "succoth" (tabernacle) for the harvest festival.

The country has all gone now and the smell of the country is gone too. And the ghetto, and all the Jews in it, are gone. It was a nice ghetto, a self-made one as people tended to crowd together surrounded with friendly, even admiring, English faces; interested faces too. We had never heard of anti-semitism, and wouldn't have known what it was. It was not just that we Russians or Poles from the "hame", as they called Eastern Europe then, were assimilated with the Brummies or anything like that. We were not assimilated; we were special. We were the favourites, the favoured citizens; we were one of the things that made the town different, like the Town Hall and the Art gallery or the jewellery quarter where they used to make swords in the old days.

When I was eleven years old I won a prize for writing an essay. That did it. From then on I was the one marked down by Father to get his family saga written.

First, though, he said I had to get a training for it, as Charles Dickens did and Arnold Bennett and people like that. So from time to time Father sat down and wrote letters to newspaper editors saying that he had a daughter who wrote poems in her room at night and who, he felt, ought to be considered for apprenticeship. But nothing ever came of it, which is just as well, because then it might have come out that I only ever wrote two poems and Father had never actually read them.

The essay prize was a great disappointment to me. All the council schoolchildren of Birmingham were taken to see a Shakespeare production at the "Alec", which was the old Alexandra Theatre. And our headmistress said the prize would be money, about £10, enough for a holiday in France or anywhere, in those days. None of us had ever been farther than Rhyl or Llandudno or Prestatyn, which were easy to reach along the Bristol Road, so that the essay competition was very tempting for us. Instead the prize was books, and mine turned out to be a big volume of the poems of Walter de la Mare. A man making the presentation came out on the platform at the "Alec" and made some excuse about the money. It put me off poetry and Shakespeare after that.

I was then at a council school in Tindall Street, which was just near Cannon Hill Park. My parents sent me there for not working or learning anything at the refined school opposite where we lived, called Edgbaston College.

Two of my sisters, Beryl and Cora, were told they might have to leave Edgbaston College also, because I might pick up a Birmingham accent at the council school and bring it home. It killed you socially, in those days, if you had a regional accent, especially a Black Country one. I wondered what the College headmistress, Miss Polly Bailey, and her deputy, Miss O'Loughlin, would have thought of Grandma's accent, which wasn't like anything and had no grammar to it, not even in Russian. Not that the two ladies ever met. Father said that was one of the things about Grandma; she was a terrible snob and didn't believe in meeting anybody at all if she could help it.

However, after that I started to keep a journal instead of writing sentimental poems. I wrote down the things that Father said, mostly. Afterwards it became a habit, writing in it.

I am told I had an unhappy childhood, though I wouldn't have said so myself. I agree we were like people in a play with the curtain going up and down and no proper intervals, so it was tiring. However, all my aunts on both sides of the family said it was unhappy. I suppose they were referring to our parents' quarrels, and then our losing our money and going from the big house to the poor cottage. After that we were always being sued for debts, and so on. In the synagogue, where we all had to go just the same, though we had to stand now through not being able to pay for a seat, or even for last year's seat, people nudged one another when they saw us. "The Poor Davises." Russian Jews, like most primitive peasant people are superstitious. Avoid unlucky people, they said to each other.

To us it seemed rather an exciting childhood, full of drama. However, I have always found that you can never stop other people from being sorry for you if they have really made up their minds about it.

Nowadays it is believed that parents who don't get on should be divorced and live separately for the sake of the children and their peace of mind. I think that is terrible nonsense. In between the rows there were glorious reconciliations. Sometimes it ended with a big party, and all of us going off together to the theatre or music-hall. I was convinced, though, that no theatre could ever compete with the drama always going on at home.

Mother liked sitting at the piano and singing "Pale hands I love beside the Shalimar". She had a nice voice. Father could be heard from far off in the bathroom or lavatory, singing . . . "If she belonged to me, I'd let 'er know 'oos 'oo." He came into the kitchen where the table was being set for lunch, wearing cheap pyjamas of a rather flashy blue, with the jacket wide open exposing an immense white chest.

Mother said, "I don't know why I ever married you. If only I'd listened to Mother. When I think of the offers I had from fine, respectable men."

"Do you mean those sissies who came to your Ma's house for the poetry readings with your sister Ray?" said Father. Aunt Ray was a schoolteacher in Higher Broughton, Salford, who had been at school with Louis Golding.

Both parents had, for us, this gift of making past and present into one continuous drama. Also, we felt that they were both much younger than we were. The trouble was that later on, in our teens, we found that girls and boys of our own ages seemed dull companions compared with our parents.

Only the twin boys kept out of the way, silent, morose. "They are like your mad Uncle Yasha," Mother said. This always started a row.

"And what about your brothers Harold and Stanley?" Harold was killed in the First World War at the age of eighteen, and Stanley had been badly shell-shocked and was entitled to be a bit odd.

One of the things that always made people feel sorry for me was because I was born in Birmingham. "I say . . . how awful. Never mind, you're not there now."

Of course, it wasn't as ugly then as it is now. Phoebe and her daughters took a dislike to the place quite early on and left the town as soon as they were able to do so, descending on it again at intervals from their chic St John's Wood address, just for weddings and funerals. Even these visits stopped eventually. I thought that Aunt Phoebe's furniture shop in Coventry Road was the most thrilling place. You could hide for hours inside the marked-down, three-piece suite or under the easy-payments super-soft bed with the fancy walnut headpiece. Beyond lay Stratford Road and the open country. I couldn't understand why Roz and Rita hated it all so much. But they were literary girls like Aunt Becky. They ran our local dramatic society, staging plays by Barrie and Shaw or musical productions like "No No Nanette".

The uncles never came to see us on account of being "broiguss" with Father, which meant not on terms. But all our cousins came in droves to play billiards in our golden-oak billiard-room, to eat Mother's chopped liver, to hear Father play the flute or recite *The Ballad of Reading Gaol*. We also had a gramophone with a huge horn which played "Hungarian Rhapsody" or "Valencia" or "Yes, we have no bananas". We had speakers in each room whereby you blew hard down a tube which whistled in another room in another wing of the house, then you put it to your ear and listened. Father loved every gadget going; he was photographed riding the first motor-cycle ever seen in Bristol Street. Above all we had our own cinematograph show, with Father turning a handle and the early Charlie Chaplin films appearing on a sheet which we hung across the nursery wall. All the neighbours and local children and all the servants crowded in to watch, and no one ever loved it half as much as Father did. This—our rich period—lasted six or seven years.

Each summer our garden blossomed with giant bluebells, wild pansies and roses, trees of Blenheim apples, gooseberries, raspberries, loganberries, and above all roses, roses, all in such

B

profusion that Blenheims and crab-apples rotted on the lawns for it was not possible to pick them all.

Few people could boast, as I could, that they went to school with Godfrey Winn and Lady Docker.

Father had already begun to go bankrupt, and each wing of our house, including the billiard-room, was closed in turn, but nevertheless I was sent to King Edward VI High School in New Street. Mother said it was because I was plain and must therefore have an education like Auntie Becky.

Father came to our drama society once to see Phoebe's daughters on the stage, but he didn't approve. Next time Phoebe came to our house, Father warned that Roz and Rita wouldn't get husbands that way. It was all too clever by half, in his opinion. So in this way I was brought up to believe that a girl had only one choice in life, and all else was delusion.

> "He sipped no sup and he craved no crumb
> As he sighed for the love of a lady"

sang Father as he tucked a napkin in his waistcoat and filled himself up with a bowl of pale yellow-green gefüllte fish which Mother had spent all morning chopping.

I helped her chop the horse-radish while the tears ran down my face from it. I couldn't quite see why girls went so mad about getting married when all you did afterwards was hours of chopping.

"You'll find out one day," said Mother. She said that Grandma Izvozchik tried in her old age to make up for everything by doing all the chopping for her sons, that is for Abe and Mo and Sam, but not for Father, of course, who was the bad son.

"The first time your Father took me to her house after we were engaged, I had a wonderful big hat on with a veil. She never even looked at me. She just went into the kitchen and went on chopping."

"She was only a stupid Russian peasant," said Father, "she didn't know any better. Phoebe's got no brains either. I told her to take her daughters off the stage; I told her it'll come to no good."

The three blond sons of the good son, Abe, grew up and married pretty Gentile girls.

This put our Father in a good mood for years. And our Mother, too, enjoyed the joke. She kept inviting Agnes and Daisy and the third bride to supper in our house, to hear over again what Uncle Abe had said, when he heard.

These were the times when our parents were happy together, in complete harmony. The talk was all about that Abe and Mo and Sam and Becky and Phoebe and Sally. They'd all . . . wait for it! . . . come to no good in the end.

Children in love with their parents often love as lovers do, in spite of faults and failings and without hope of awaking a like response. Both parents I loved that way, but Father was an awful tease. You never knew where you were with him. He had only one set of judgments; either you took after his own sisters or, the Good Lord be praised, you didn't.

If I was in favour then I was like "poor Auntie Rose". Auntie Rose had died tragically young. This was the sort of story he always liked, as it was romantic and tearful and he could sing sentimental verses about it. In fact Rose had married a tall Pole, a rather crabby man we called Uncle Lou who sold mackintoshes and umbrellas and who was always very gloomy if it didn't rain. His name was Rainbow. His business, rather like our own Father's, was always going "bust", so the rainfall in the Midlands must have been quite inadequate in those days after the First World War. However, when Rosie died Lou acquired a stepmother for his children and this provided my parents with endless pleasure. For the stepmother turned out to be rather old and cold and strict with the babies left in her charge and this made an even better story for

Father than little Rosie in the Grimsby gutters singing sad Russian songs, with her tiny hand held out.

I prayed not to be like Aunt Phoebe because, Father said, she was the worst. On the second exodus from Russia there was not enough train fare for everyone, unless Phoebe, who was nearly seven, could pretend she was under five, and therefore travel free of charge.

When the ticket-collector came to examine the rather scruffy lot in a third class compartment, he soon tired of trying to sort them out because no one seemed able to speak anything except Russian or Yiddish and those who could wisely kept quiet. He was just about to leave them in peace with a warning nod at one small bundle, saying, "As long as she's under five then that's all right." These, intact, were the words handed down to us, as history by Father, who claimed never to forget a single word that his relations ever spoke.

But Phoebe was the smart one, the one who'd soon picked up English again during the time spent in Grimsby after the landing. "Ah'm over six," said Phoebe to the ticket-collector, and it marked her for life. Grandfather, who had to walk most of the way to Birmingham after that ("It was snowing" Father said with relish), never spoke to Phoebe again. So, on my bad days, I was like "Auntie Phoebe who just couldn't keep her big mouth shut". It left its mark on me too. I didn't learn to keep my mouth shut, but I learned to know in advance that it was asking for trouble, each and every time I opened it.

To hear Father say you were just like your Auntie Becky meant you would probably never get a boy-friend. And to be like Auntie Sally meant you were a cry-baby.

In fact, it was Auntie Phoebe who made a real success by getting married to an industrious man she met in the cabinet-making French-polishing business. They had all been so anxious to get rid of Phoebe that they apprenticed her in childhood, first to her eldest brother Abe, who apprenticed her to someone else. But instead of talking herself out of a job as everyone expected, Phoebe was as nice to the customers as she was nasty—and who could blame her?—at home with the family. Soon Phoebe was rich and married the son of the boss and had three children of her own. So then Father hated her more than ever, and Phoebe was hardly ever invited to our Mother's card evenings with music. And, of course, Auntie Phoebe hated us too, which meant we now had three aunts and three uncles with whom we were "not speaking".

In those days, I think, people used to get much more fun out of each other than they do now. They had lots of friends to whom they were absolutely devoted, with three or four visits to each other's homes per week, and one card evening with music at least once a month, or even more. And most people had friends or relations with whom they had quarrelled and were not speaking, and so there was never any shortage of topics for conversation or gossip.

When Father lost his business for the third or fourth time and had to go cap in hand, so to speak, to his eldest brother Abe, to ask for money for a loan, Auntie Phoebe had plenty to talk about. She took quite a fancy to us then and started calling on us without even being invited. It was all part of the game of life as it was lived then, in a narrow provincial circle of once poor immigrants like us. It was just Auntie Phoebe's turn to have some fun at our expense, and to be quite fair it was a fun to which she was by this time really entitled.

Perhaps it was just that the old, old habits of terrible poverty are never really forgotten. Certainly Father, who had, so he said, practically starved to death up to the age of fourteen, remained hungry all his life. He never ate a meal so much as wolfed it, and even if it were a four course meal with all the trimmings he never left a crumb on any plate.

One day, on my way home from school, I encountered a

breathless Auntie Phoebe in the road. Whether on speaking terms or not, all the Poor Davises lived within a square mile radius of one another, which meant that they often passed each other in silence in the road, or had to climb upstairs in the tramcar to avoid having to say "Good morning, Abe".

"I've got something for all of you children," said Auntie Phoebe in a kindly tone to me. "Something special." We all knew that Phoebe and her family were moving house and going somewhere better and bigger. "Take these home to your Mother. It's a present from your Aunt Phoebe. No, don't thank me. Nichevo, child, nichevo!" Auntie Phoebe liked to show she'd not forgotten all her Russian.

I ran home with the little packet to show to Mother. Inside the paper-bag was about half a pound of broken biscuits of the duller sort, just plain ones. Not even with icing on top or a single currant layer. They were the broken remains of some cheap stale biscuits left lying in a drawer, anywhere away from mice.

Mother threw them in the dustbin and then went out to the yard to retrieve them. They must be spread out on a plate to show to Father when he got home.

In fact we kept those biscuits for weeks so that they could be shown to visitors. "Have I ever told you the story," said Father as the visitors arrived, specially summoned to see Aunt Phoebe's present, "of my sister Phoebe on the train after we got back from Russia the second time?"

In the end the bits of broken biscuit were given to our youngest sister Bettina, who was only four, so that she could feed them to her dolls. At the end of that week they were all gone at last, crumbled to nothing, but our 'Tina could still be heard muttering to herself: "Ah'm over six, over six."

Our Mother, eldest of five daughters, had a special fear and horror of any daughter of hers remaining unmarried. If our friends or neighbours had unmarried daughters, Mother behaved to them with a sort of hushed sympathy as though there were sickness in the house.

So when it came to choosing a career for each of her own four daughters, of which I was the second, we had to bear in mind, she said, that there were certain kinds of jobs which men didn't like girls doing, and there were also those they didn't mind about.

Teaching, for example, was thought to be risky in those days. Several of her friends had been teachers and had married dangerously late, about 24 or 25 and then not very suitably in her opinion. On the other hand no reasonable husband could, she felt, complain that teaching in any way damaged a girl as wife-material. Possibly the Civil Service was the best bet, with the attraction of special pension rights.

It was not that our Mother was not romantic. On the contrary, she knew herself to be very much so, which meant that she must take herself in hand when insuring our futures by guiding us as surely as possible towards a life of unending, unclouded married bliss, which she knew existed because she'd read so much about it in library novels.

She worried especially about me, and about my being a hockey-playing schoolgirl who was often left hanging about at dances.

"I'm only eighteen," I said sulkily. "I've got time left, haven't I?"

But Mother only sighed and said:

"There's never enough time; a girl always has to worry."

Mother one day handed me a new book she'd got from the library. It was a new novel by E. M. Delafield called *Thank heaven fasting*. No need to ask her what a girl had to thank heaven for.

"Your Father worries about you," Mother said, "in case you turn out like your Aunt Phoebe or Aunt Becky."

My ambitions to be a writer and journalist were becoming a great source of anxiety to her. Somehow she felt instinctively—and later I was to find how right she was—that men didn't really care for writing-women. It made them, she felt, rather nervous. For one thing, writing-women might, quite unintentionally of course, give a man the impression that she thought she knew all the answers. And no self-respecting man would stand for that, or contemplate getting married to it.

Perhaps this may sound absurd today, but for us, in those remote days between the two wars, it was a very real anxiety, especially as the twenties turned into the thirties and business got worse everywhere and wars began to break out in so many places one after the other. Nearly every young girl had a spinster auntie—and I certainly had—whose lover or boy had never come back from the First World War.

So, from about age fifteen onwards, life became very exhausting for us girls. Mother insisted that we should join all the local clubs, take part in literary debates and turn up at local rambles and tennis parties, dances, etc. Instead of hockey, or just lolling about with a book on Saturday afternoons as in the old days, you had to get your hair washed and try on various dresses to see which Mother liked you best in, or more likely didn't like at all. Then in the early hours of the morning, just worn to a frazzle, you had to be brought home by Father in his old Ford car in time to tell her who had asked you to dance or for tennis or skating next time. There was just never any let-up.

It was humiliating the way Father was never in a hurry, even at 2 a.m., to drive us girls home in the car. He liked to hang about to see if I had made any "conquests". If so, the conquest could be encountered getting his coat or coming out of the Gents' and offered a lift, "if he's going our way home". Not many lads had their own cars in those days, and Father knew full well that many an enterprising boy would have the sense to snatch the last dance with me, in the hope of being invited to share in a lift home.

The trouble was I had no luck at dances, being awkward at the whole sport of getting boys to dance with me, whereas at hockey and swimming I could really shine. At eighteen, however, I stopped a hockey ball with my mouth, taken at full spin from somebody's illicitly raised stick. "The only time," said Father, "that our Olyechka had her big mouth shut." He invited everyone into the kitchen to witness that it would be my last game ever. Snapping my stick, with but little trouble, across his knee, for he was an immensely strong man, Father said, "No nice boy likes to be seen dancing with a girl wearing a purple and green moustache." It took a month or more for my hockey bruise to fade away.

The arrival of several American medical students, who found it cheaper to take a degree at our local university than at home, caused a little stir in our town. They were a novelty to us provincial girls then, in 1929, the year of *Broadway Melody* and talkies and general excitement about everything from over there. Ben, Joe and Harry were attractive too, and much in demand for socials and so on. Everyone was surprised at Ben, the big, blond one, picking me out for dancing. "It must be a magic spell," Father said, "or maybe the lad needs glasses."

Father was referring, of course, to my complexion, which wasn't good. Everything had been tried. The night before a dance I came out in an assortment of purple spots. Psychiatrists had not yet been thought of in our world, at least not in the circles in which we moved. No one suspected I might be just allergic to the misery of dances, dodging between the buffet and the merciful secrecy of the lavatory where no one could notice that I had not yet achieved a partner. Instead, it was believed, I had bad blood. I had to be purged with lickorish powder, castor oil and worse, with the result that even more horrible rashes burst out as though in rage at the disturbance created inside me.

My parents were not the kind to give in so easily. Where castor oil might fail, cosmetics could be tried. They were still in a comparatively primitive state, and not usually applied to very young girls unless they were among the fast set. But Father, who studied chemistry on his own, and even at one time launched a successful business on the strength of his own patented hair oil, saw a way to turn me, if not into a beauty, into something nearer to his own distinctive taste.

One night it was decided, much against my wish, to paint me white all over before the dance, with a kind of cream paste so thick that almost every blemish, including moles and spots, would be concealed. A white skin like alabaster was very much to Father's taste, and he thought this was a marvellous way of disguising his second daughter's sallow and blemished skin.

Everyone at home came to watch the operation, which seemed to go on forever. It was the fashion for low-backed and décolleté dresses for evening wear. Before enclosing me firmly in my orange satin gown, I was painted all over the back, arms and neck and emerged as a dazzling, uncomfortable figure like some marble statue. Father was in raptures over me. A real "film" girl I looked, Father said. He admired film stars like Joan and Constance Bennett and especially Marlene Dietrich, and it was his considered opinion that now I "looked more like it". We all considered Father to be something of an expert on the difficult subject of sex, by virtue of the many temptations to which he had so readily succumbed. We all of us, therefore, listened with some respect to his assessment of our sexual attractions, feeling that in this regard, at least, his opinion must be authoritative and informed.

It was hot in the big dance hall, where a large crowd were already fox-trotting to tunes from *Broadway Melody*. "Gosh," said Ben removing his hand from my bare back, since after all there was no orange satin covering for him to rest his hand on, "you're all sticky. Gawd, kid, what is it?" Alas, my dazzling make-up was melting fast.

But there was worse to come.

"Hi, Ben," shouted Harry, "you're turning white all over. What's the matter with you, man?"

Ben stood there in the middle of the floor looking at the arms and jacket of his black evening jacket, now all white as though dipped in flour. The tune "Putting on the Ritz" followed me in my headlong dash to the safety of the "Ladies".

Ben came to our house for tea next day. People always did go on coming for tea to us, no matter what, because of Mother's cheesecake and chopped liver, and dinner afterwards was even better.

Father thought the story of how Ben turned white at the dance was a jolly good story. Not as good as Aunt Phoebe on the train, of course, but good enough. He and Ben became good friends after that, because as it turned out they were both interested in all kinds of experiments. Ben said he wanted to study psychiatry after taking a medical degree, and Father told him all about our Aunt Becky, and how he'd tried hard to turn me into a success at dances so that I wouldn't be like her and have to wait years and years for a beau.

This was not, however, the only one of Father's "inventions" which were to melt away, so to speak, before his very eyes. Night after night he sat up until the dawn—inventing something new that was going to make all our fortunes, and save him from bankruptcy. He invented and himself made a laundry steriliser equipped with formaldehyde container, a springless mattress, a corner wardrobe, a carousel-coffee-table. Meanwhile we got poorer every day.

We always obeyed our parents in those days, so that life then seemed one long round of terrifying dances and social occasions. It took me long years to refuse invitations without feeling guilty about it.

The debating-hall of our local tennis and cultural club filled up early with the few confident ones. Then came the humbler sort, ambitious to copy this kind of confidence. And late as possible, in hope that the proceedings might really be almost over, we arrived, looking fearfully neither to right nor to left, stumbling to a seat, trying not to overhear those whispers.

"Look who's come . . ."

"She must have heard Julius was coming tonight."

"HE would never look at HER."

From the corner of a reluctant eye I'd spotted Cedric, who was my only conquest of the season. Poor Cedric, he had a lisp, a spotty face and a dreadful giggle. Cedric's mother used to go about with a hunted look as though people blamed her.

"Cedric's looking at you," Cora said. Cora was nearly as pretty as our eldest sister Beryl, and, if not entirely confident, at least relaxed. At sixteen she didn't have to worry as I did.

"Shut UP!"

"No need to be nasty."

I crept into bed at night beside my little sister 'Tina.

It seemed as though life were empty of beauty and full of dis-illusion. I had stopped writing poetry. I could hear the Henry Hall band playing over the radio, as I slid into sleep, "Good night, sweetheart". I didn't enjoy being young. It was really too much of a worry, the whole thing.

"I'm afraid," said Father at breakfast, "Ogg's going to be another Auntie Becky."

What bad luck to be young just then, instead of experiencing the thrills, the hardships my parents had. I thought of Babushka trudging the snow, pregnant, wrapped in shawls, climbing the slippery, oily gangway and on to the rocking boat for England. Father said, "We sold newspapers and matches in Smallbrook Street. Even in winter we often went barefoot." It wasn't fair that he should have been so lucky. It had been full of drama for him, going barefoot like Hans Andersen's Little Matchseller, and that burning glow of the last matchbox turning the snow to purple.

I hated Babushka for leaving Russia. I'd been robbed of a life, woods under snow, wolves and even bears, going to school on horseback. And above all people. My sort of people, speaking my language. Pushkin, or Lermontov seeing a "lonely white sail on the ocean".

"Don't be silly," Father said. "People have to go where their living is. Or where the next generation's living is. It was all right for her, but what about my Father having to live with in-laws? You know what I think about relations."

Father didn't mind my speaking Russian or any other language, as long as I didn't speak it too well. "Don't get clever, like your Aunt Becky," he said, "there's nothing worse than a clever woman."

It had been his responsibility to introduce Becky to a suitor; to escort her to dances and parties. "She'd make a beeline for the oldest, boringest professor in the room, so they could admire how clever she was."

Alas, the professors were also married. And Becky was already twenty-seven. Father was the local wolf. As a lad he'd worked for big brother Abe in his furniture shop. He was successful at persuading customers that the shop was full of genuine antiques and other valuable furniture. Father was good-looking, with his crisp blond hair and ginger moustache, and he was also successful at persuading the local shopgirls to climb over the back wall with him and lie down among the empty showcases or even on the ground. Now he felt ready to settle down if only he could get Becky fixed up. Grandma was on to him all the time about it. Find a beau for Becky. You must not think of marrying anyone until Becky's suited.

Babushka didn't really like her son Izzy. He wasn't, she knew, quite respectable, but more like one of those savages from the

Russian steppes; as a child he never said his prayers unless she beat him until she was exhausted. But Grandma was ready to make friends with Izzy if it meant a hope of getting Becky wed.

Father couldn't stand Becky; she had opinions; she talked well and often. She had been the first of the Poor Davises ever to go to a university.

So in the end he got married first. That did it. Grandma always walked past our house without calling after that. If our Mother called on her, she went into the kitchen and wouldn't speak.

There never was a time when every member of the family was speaking. So no wonder Abe wore an air of tired melancholy and Mo used to go about saying, "My God, what a rotten lot we are."

Mo corresponded with a burglar. He liked people who were "different" and "original", and he considered it was an interesting experience to go to prison. He used to send the burglar letters and parcels in prison. Then he got affectionate and grateful letters back. I suspected that the burglar filled the place of the brother Mo would like to have had. No one could say the Poor Davis brothers were ever affectionate or grateful. We were like some beleaguered tribe surrounded by hostile tribes who would destroy us if they could gain entry to our nest.

In the end it was not Father but the youngest of the family, Aunt Sally Davis, who found a husband for Becky.

Aunt Sally had the unenviable job of being secretary to Mo and Izzy, who jointly founded a business manufacturing razor-blades and shaving-brushes.

One day Ernest Adler arrived from Pilsen in Czechoslovakia to do business, and took a fancy to young Sally.

She wasn't much of a Poor Davis. She was a pale, sad girl with a long-suffering air of self-sacrifice. This was explained by her position as intermediary and employee between all the warring brothers. (Sally is the only one left now of the former

Izvozchik family, and she won't thank me for saying that, whatever she tried to do to bring peace among the brothers, she never had a hope.) In those days, no one understood the difficulties of communication between members of large families once forced to live cramped together in one or two tiny rooms, sleeping four or even five to a bed. She was intelligent enough to recognise that the Poor Davises burned with all the primitive passions, hate, envy, jealousy, and worse still the love-hate of those who understand one another but would rather die than admit it. She was a fragile girl, and it was all too much for her. She told Herr Ernest Adler how to find her clever sister Becky, who had an interpreter's job in London. In no time at all Becky was a bride, and we never saw her until 1939, when the Adlers had to flee from the Nazi Germans.

We had never seen her until then. But she lived with us from day to day, in Father's family saga. They sat with us, in our imagination, at our family table, all the wicked uncles, the much too clever aunts.

Suddenly, the razor and shaving-brush business was paying. We were rich. We moved to a big house on the Bristol Road. It lasted six years. The worst years, I thought. Being rich didn't really suit us. Father got wilder than ever.

Mother gave large parties in the light oak billiard-room. Far away, in the girls' bedroom, we sniffed hungrily at the aroma of bitter chocolates in silver dishes, dates stuffed with almonds and rolled in chopped coconut, anchovy eggs. The party played poker, solo and bridge at small tables, murmuring to each other. Where was the host? Where was that mad Russian villain, the one who made them scream, and told those terribly risqué stories? They wanted to hear more of the wicked uncles, the snooty aunties. Was it true that Abe had a mistress and illegitimate children and a whole, wholly other interesting life? What a family, what a lot!

Mother would be busy, busy, pretending that she was not

listening with concentrated, agonised patience for the sound of his key in the door, the rough cough, and then . . . the entrance that would turn this quite ordinary party into a riot.

When he came, it was already a few minutes past midnight. The guests, restless, had been asking for coats, preparing to go home because it was too late. Now they settled expectantly in their chairs, reached for a drink or a chocolate. At last. He might enter wearing our black cat across his shoulders and a damaged soldier's cap left by one of our uncles who had served in the Great War, and be Barnaby Rudge. Or he would rummage in the cloak-room and find a cloak, a Homburg hat, and be Oscar Wilde. Or he would be Frank Harris, Horatio Bottomley, or most likely nowadays he would come in as Chaplin or Mr Micawber or Mr Jingle, or snatch a sheet from our beds and be the Sheikh of Araby, who was very popular that year.

However, the money did not last very long. Soon our home was sold up, including all our books and furniture, and we went to live in a tiny cottage on the Bourneville estate. Of course, being poor in those days was not so uncomfortable as it is today. You could buy fresh food in cheap, open-air markets and cook it your-self, which meant we were better off than in the big house where the servants' quarter was so far away that the food was cold when it reached us, and not very good anyway because Cook was always leaving or the housemaid was, so that often the food never got as far as the nursery at all. In our tiny cottage the walls fairly rocked with the heat as long as we had enough coal or slack for the stove, whereas in the big house we froze because the radiators were always breaking down and it was a major operation to get coal for fires in every room.

Mother started to shop at the Co-op, and was so good at making ends meet and saving up her dividend that soon she had a little sum which she was able to put in a box and hide under the mattress in the girls' room so that Father would not find it.

He went to Germany to try and sell his springless mattress, and came back full of admiration for the Germans. They were so sophisticated and progressive. The schoolgirls carried their own contraceptive kit in their satchels, said Father, after visiting Hamburg.

"Do you have to . . . in front of the children?" Mother said. She said that now he was at home he had better talk to Olyechka about her behaviour at the weekend summer school camp at Colwyn Bay. Instead of taking part in the normal boy and girl petting parties, I had gone about with an elderly, bearded professor and talked about Russia.

Father said it was Aunt Becky all over again, but he promised to talk to me about it.

I was eighteen, and the oddest thing had happened. During Father's absence, some of the long-lost uncles had started to call at Mother's invitation. Mother still had hopes of a modest loan from Uncle Abe if the right kind of approach were made. I knew the uncles well by sight, of course, but it was the first time I had actually spoken to them or handed them a plate of chopped herring or cheesecake.

Father, too, was amazed. "What, here?" he said. "Coming here?" The snag was that Uncle Abe and Uncle Mo, who were willing to be reconciled with brother Izzy who was now too poor to be any sort of competition, were certainly not willing to be reconciled with each other. Mother said we should put them side by side at the family tea-table to avoid their having to catch sight of each other when asking someone to pass the cheesecake.

There were always, as I have said, distinct advantages in being poor. Father was undoubtedly now the slimmest of the brothers. We watched with interest how the uncles carefully negotiated their bellies underneath the table as they drew chairs up to the table.

"And how was Germany?" said Abe.

"Wunderschön," said Father, who, alas, had little of Aunt Becky's aptitude for German grammar but had all her talent for showing off.

"Did you do any Geschäft in Germany?" said Mo, not to be outdone either in German grammar or in conversational ploys.

"Not quite wunderschön enough," said Father gamely, carefully maintaining the fiction that only ONE of his two brothers was actually present.

"I'd like a chat with you about it after tea," said Abe.

"I might call back this evening for a little chat about it," said Mo.

Our Mother, with great tact and not a little enjoyment, had provided two separate dishes for the various cakes and sandwishes, to avoid the embarrassment of the brothers having to help themselves from the same plate.

CHAPTER IV

LOOKING FOR WORK

Now that Father had no money at all, we all had to leave school and go to work. Father was hoping I would get a job as a reporter on a newspaper and learn how to be a writer. But how to start? Nobody knew.

Instead I went to work in factories, taking dictation in shorthand in German and sometimes in French, translating German blueprints into English. No one, of course, in those days wanted a knowledge of Russian.

I was fired from one motor-cycle factory for bad German grammar. I didn't know, sobbing into the pillow, which thing I dreaded most; telling Father or getting a week's notice from the elderly Swiss.

"Stop yelling," Father said, "he's not going to put a good British girl out of work and get a Swiss one. Oh no, I shall write to the Home Office and get the work permit stopped."

I stopped crying and implored Father to let well alone. The Swiss might be horrible, but so was my German grammar.

"Take this letter," Father said, and I sat down at his typewriter, still weeping. I always had to type his letters when I got home from work.

"The Home Office should hear about this," Father said importantly, "firing a good British girl for a foreign one at a time like this."

It was 1931. There were a lot of Britishers out of work now, apart from me. About two million, all told. Still, it was embarrassing. What sort of Britishers are we, I said, with our Russian relations and a name picked for us by a Welsh schoolmaster out of the Welsh valleys and not ours at all?

"You do as I say," Father said, "and don't argue with your Father."

In no time at all, back came the letter from the Home Office praising Father for his timely report. Back I must go to the New Hudson Motor-cycle Company in Hockley. Permission could not be granted for a Swiss girl to get a permit in view of the unemployment situation.

Father was always saying I was too outspoken, like Aunt Phoebe, as well as having the dangerous likeness to Aunt Becky. A girl had to hide things, not only her brains either. You shouldn't, Father said, go about showing people you'd just lost a tooth, even if it was only a back tooth. That was not the way to get a husband.

Then, suddenly, I had a young man of my own. Father kept on about it day and night.

"You didn't have to tell him you'd got flat feet," said Father when I was clearing away the tea-things from the table.

I felt terribly anxious. It was clear to me, without Father's mentioning it, that such an interesting and attractive young man could hardly have any serious intentions towards me, even if my feet were not flat, which they were.

"You're mad, Father," I said, because now we were older we often said things to his face which we should never have dared to say before. For one thing, since our Mother's death a few months earlier we all knew that Father was sleeping with our housekeeper, a blonde young woman with a baby who had come to us from the local Salvation Army home. Father said rude things about her to us when she was out of the room, but that didn't stop him.

"No, it's your young man who's mad. A good-looking, personable fellow like that; he could have anybody."

I thought rather gloomily that it was probably Father whom my young man came to visit, rather than me. He hadn't seemed to mind when I went to bed early one night, leaving him with Father. They sat the whole night drinking and talking. Hadn't it always been the same? All our visitors came to see him and hear him. Father was a good talker. "A plausible rascal," our Mother had called him.

I remembered the day the bailiffs came to take all our furniture away. I let them in the back door because I'd just come in from school and there was no one else at home. I watched them going round our kitchen, writing down in a notebook the value of each item, which wasn't much. Father had walked straight into it. Hours later, he'd talked them into going away and coming back next day. He was triumphant. "Food for fishes," he sang gaily as I made the tea, and he kept slapping me on the back, happy as though he hadn't a care in the world. When the bailiffs did return next day, several important items were already gone, and Father with them.

Now the brothers, after a lifetime of fighting, were meeting more and more often at our house. We could not get used to the novelty of it. The youngest brother Sam, who had served in the army, incredibly enough, as a Captain, had fled to South Africa rather than pay the income tax on some diamond deal. Now only Abe and Mo and Izzy were left.

The old animosity and hatred had cooled in middle age to a rueful, ironic tolerance. Abe now saw Izzy as an amiable eccentric, a happy-go-lucky rascal, but he still shrank from actual contact or converse with Mo. Luckily we still had two adjoining rooms, a big kitchen opening out into a sitting-room. Usually now, on a Saturday afternoon, Abe would fill the armchair in one, while Mo sat or plodded heavy-footed round the other. My sisters and I plied between them bearing plates of food.

Why the brothers came, after nearly a lifetime of staying away, was never explained. To me, it seemed, they all felt uneasy without the motive force of battle and competitiveness that had always raged between them. Now they regarded each other, sometimes silently, with curiosity. They were like disgruntled married partners who can be happy neither together nor apart, and who come together as though searching for something they once had and then lost.

Uncle Abe, to my acute embarrassment, was taking an interest in my fragile love affair. Would it, he wanted to know from Father, come to a deal? Or would the young man take flight when he became aware of our position, which was that our home and everything in it was finally due to be sold over our heads at any moment, to pay our debts?

Father just laughed, though without his usual gaiety. He no longer cared what Abe thought.

Uncle Mo was beckoning from the other room. What were those madmen saying? No doubt Abe was flaunting his money as usual. "How vulgar," said Mo. "I would never do a thing like that. I may not have his thousands, but I've not done too badly. Not badly at all. Did I tell you girls," said Mo, "how I ran away to sea when I was a boy and went to America? I had to get away from those bastards; they were always on to me, always chucking me out of bed, trying to beat me up. I wasn't more than fourteen. Have I told you?"

Yes, he had told us. However, here it was again.

CHAPTER V

LOOKING FOR LOVE

ONE OF THE bonds between Father and my young man Norbert was the understanding of what it meant to be an immigrant, with no name, no country. To have at least five brothers, with a different language and background.

Norbert arrived in our town from Paris, where he had been living with his brother Rudolf, who had a leather business called Frenkel Frères. Rudolf had still another brother working for him named Henri, just as Uncle Abe had once employed our Father.

Listening to Norbert telling us his story, it seemed that life was repeating itself. Except that for the "poor Izvozchiks" hunger and cold had been the only enemies. Not so for the Frenkel Frères, trapped in Russian Poland.

Norbert was born in Lodz, a kind of Manchester. Again as in Grandpa's case, it was the wife and mother, while bearing six sons and a daughter, who earned the family living and virtually kept the scholarly husband, who did little work but spent his time in praying or teaching his sons to pray. She had a little workroom making articles in linen.

I knew that I was in love when he said he would come to tea on Saturday. It was my birthday.

"If he brings a present," Father said, "I shall have to speak to him. You can't accept it, not unless it's flowers."

Everyone at our dinner table rocked with laughter, and I heard them, miserably. Perhaps he wouldn't come anyway. He might forget. Or he might talk it over with his brother and decide it might be too compromising to come to my birthday tea, in front of all the uncles and some aunts as well. They were coming for the chopped herring and cheesecake, and anything else that might be on the table. Cooking was about the only talent our Mother had passed on to us. Clever mothers hardly ever have clever daughters, because all the daughters can do is just look on, admiring or despairing. But cook we could, and the uncles, who seemed to be always hungry, knew it. Father said all immigrants who had had years of starvation were like this. Food wasn't just a meal; it gave you a sense of achievement just to eat it.

I was employed at that time in the export department of Joseph Lucas, who supplied all the electrical accessories, like headlamps and batteries, for motor-cars. A little group of us took dictation in French, German or Spanish in shorthand adapted to the language. "Is he really coming for your birthday on Saturday? Can I come? I do want to see what he's like." This was my friend Paula, who worked in the same factory.

I said yes, of course, but I was shuddering inwardly. Everyone was counting on it and talking about it as though it were real. And it wasn't real at all. I knew better than they did what life was really like. I remembered evenings, sitting fresh from a bath, in my best dress with a big bow in my hair; all of us looking at the table, set like a banquet, salted almonds, the smell of fresh rye loaf under a white cloth, the bowl of cold halibut in egg and lemon sauce, fried plaice on the bone, rolled sweet herrings in sour cream, the freshly chopped horse-radish, the white and the red.

We were waiting for our Father, staring at the food and the flowers, giggling softly, sneaking an almond. Half-past seven. At 8.30 one of the boys was sent to his room for rudeness. He wound up our nursery gramophone and I could hear it faintly. "All alone by the telephone, waiting for a ring from you. All alone, I'm so all alone." After that we ate our supper, but we were not hungry any more and not much was eaten. At 9.30 we were sent to bed. A long time afterwards the sound of the front door woke me, and I didn't get to sleep again for a long time. First there was shouting, then silence. For a long time I could hear the sound of someone crying.

Paula was saying that Saturday afternoon that she hoped he would come soon, before she had to go.

Father said, "These Continentals never realise that English tea is at four o'clock."

"When do I get my tea?" said Uncle Abe, shifting his belly restlessly on his knees. He looked awkward in those silly chairs we had in our living-room, just off the kitchen. But the room was too small for more than one armchair.

Next door Uncle Mo was making the cane armchair squeak as he shifted about by the kitchen fire.

"I seem to know that voice," said Uncle Mo, with his deep throaty giggle. Now and then, just for the hell of it, he strolled into the other room, very daring, prowling round, tapping the copper warming-pan on the wall. "Where d'you get this damn thing?"

Not one pale eyelash on Uncle Abe quivered. He sat like some obese Rodin statue, one elbow supported on his knee, small, gloomy blue eyes fixed upon the table. Beryl's mother-in-law had made us a dish of chopped chicken's liver and I had spread it trimly on bridge rolls, with cress and crumbled egg.

Father put the kettle on the stove, murmuring, "I shan't let you play in our garden, I don't love you any more . . .'

Having done his little dare, Mo wandered back, slightly bored now and clearly longing for some action. "What will your young man make of our lunatic lot?"

Father said "Don't start anything, Mo, will you? Not while Oggi's beau is here."

"Start something with Abie?" Mo said. "He only gives me the creeps. He's lonely, I suppose, the poor bugger. He's a snob, too. I've just thought it all out. All that money's made him a snob. Do

I get snobbish? I've got money too. Not so much, but enough."

I thought this pretty tactless, considering that Father and the rest of us had none at all, and did not know which way to turn to get some.

"Babushka was a snob," said Father. "Remember our Mamenka with her fourteen windows and Grandfather with his horses and his white hands. Never did a stroke of work in Russia, with all those slaves waiting on them."

"You're right, Izz," said Mo, "rotten lot of snobs."

Now that Father was completely "broke", Mo seemed, incredible as it sounded, almost fond of him. Abe too, though he offered nothing in the way of financial help, was becoming almost a close friend. They came, in some strange way, to see Father and to savour their triumph over him. And yet they were watchful, wary, as though also aware that in spite of all he had something they had not got, never had nor would have, and they could not quite fathom what it was.

Mo said, "D'you know who came to see us? That lunatic sister of ours, Phoebe! Talk about snobs. A flat in St John's Wood. Holidays in Juan-les-Pins. What a bag she is, going all to pieces. Poor silly bitch."

"Ah'm over six," said Father. "I thought they'd kill her."

Mo was enjoying himself. He loved this kind of reminiscence. "We're a lovely lot." To me he said, "If your beau's got any sense he'll keep away." He brought a letter from his pocket. "Who do you think writes to me now? Our long-lost brother, Sam. He'd like to come home, he says." Mo choked with laughter. "Oh God, I'd like that. They'd arrest him at the docks. I could really have some fun."

There was an uneasy stirring and coughing in the next room. Abe had heard this. He couldn't speak because that would be just what Mo would want, an admission of Mo's existence, right there in the next room, in the flesh, the solid flesh. But it was clear from that loud rough cough that our Uncle Abe did not approve of Uncle Sam returning home and getting himself arrested. Abe was a Grand Master of some high Masonic order and a pillar of respectability in spite of having one extra wife and family, which could happen, we felt, to anybody.

Meanwhile it was nearly five o'clock. I was thinking—perhaps I shall die quite young. I do hope so. How terrible to live for years and hear people say about the marvellous man who'd seemed so keen on her and then one day he stopped coming to the house. I could hear them say, "Do you know, that poor girl, she aged from that very day."

Paula came in from a walk round the garden with our little sister 'Tina. "Think I'll have to go. It's getting late."

It was almost a relief to see her as far as the front door. "All right, sorry your friend didn't turn up, see you Monday," she said. Then I saw by her face as she went through the door that he was coming up the little garden path, and that she was amazed that someone like this was interested in me.

"I can stay a bit anyway," said Paula, turning back into the house.

Now I was an "engaged" girl, and I couldn't get used to it. Father was even more astonished than I was. My parents had both believed that only pretty girls could be pleasing to men, and I wasn't pretty. At that time this view of my parents seemed to me both sophisticated and justified.

It was arranged that we should spend Christmas with my fiancé's brothers and family in Paris, which was then a full day's journey from Birmingham by train and boat. I had never before been further than Colwyn Bay.

I was sure something would happen to stop the trip, and for some weeks lived in suspense. For Norbert had no passport, but only a carte d'identité from the French, and another enabling him to live in Germany. He had no more than the Home Office

permission to stay in England for such time as he was in a position
to employ a number of people in the leather industry. In the end
a permit was granted for him to go and see his family, and we
sailed that Christmas week from Dover. I was stunned with
excitement.

Dressed by Beryl, who had both taste and tact, I looked for the
first time neat and presentable. She had chosen the navy dress with
care, and tied my hair back with a bow so that, no beauty still,
I was not untidy; yet still fearful as ever. I knew there was something wrong somewhere. Life after all, I felt sure, was never
meant to be like this. I was the granddaughter of starving Russian
peasants who had begged from strangers in the streets of Grimsby.
My Father was pursued by creditors and servant-girls with pater-
nity orders. I was a rather lacklustre provincial girl working as a
German shorthand-typist. When criticised, I cried. What would
my Paris relations make of me? In those days it was harder for a
girl to cope with the sheer misery of being young, and if only the
man beside me had been less attractive I might have felt less cowed.

"Remember," Father had said, "to keep your big mouth shut.
Remember your nose gets shiny if you forget to powder it. And
if they ask you what my business is, say you're not quite sure."

The last, at least, I could honestly fulfil. But when we got to the
the Gare du Nord, and Rudolf and Anna were waiting with the
car to take us home to Boulevard Richard Le Noir in the Place de
la Bastille, they didn't have any English and my commercial
French was quite unsuitable, I quickly found, for getting on terms
with my future in-laws. It was not until I found I could not have a
bath because there was a large carp floating in it that I began to
enjoy myself. That carp made me feel at once English and
superior.

At night I lay awake in the large, tall room listening to the endless swish of traffic, and eyeing the bidet by the wall outlined by
the flashing headlights through the half open shutters. I couldn't

sleep. I struggled with the tall shutters and double windows and stood there watching the traffic through the night. Our town at home was never like this.

Tomorrow we were going to a Polish party with some neighbours, the Dudelcyks and the Halperns, and they had never met an English girl before. Afterwards Rudolf was taking us to a Christmas dinner-dance that would last the night through until champagne breakfast in the morning.

The children Ruth and Marcel came running in with their presents in the morning.

"Bonjour, Tante Olga, comment ça va! Hast Du gut 'geshluffen'?"

The nanny spoke only Russian, the grandmother only Yiddish, the parents only French and the children a mixture of all. They had never met an English girl before, they said.

Ah, if only it were true. A real English girl. I had a borrowed name and he had no country.

Next night we danced all night and drank champagne to celebrate that Christmas 1933. And I was still afraid.

We were married the following year. Big Uncle Abe, the rich one with whom we had all been at war all our lives, gave me away. Father couldn't be there in case some of his creditors turned up, but he managed to squeeze in unnoticed for the reception afterwards. Yet even now, tired, a little faded and lined, his springy fair hair dust-coloured, he could still draw the crowds of admirers. He was still the centre of attraction. I watched him go up to his brothers, our wicked uncles, our figures of fun who had suddenly turned into unexpected fairy godfathers, and I saw him, unsmiling, thank them for making a wedding for me.

The relations from Paris were dancing stylishly together. There was a buzz of aunts and cousins saying they hoped I would be happy all my life. It sounded in my ears for a long time afterwards. Happy life, happy. . . . Were they happy all their lives?

But I made a bad start, for on the second day of the honeymoon
the Paris relations arrived, to make a gay party. I was unwelcom-
ing and tearful. They had had their share of him; now it was my
turn.

I was ignorant. I knew nothing. After they had gone, a little
hurt, disappointed, Norbert said he owed them a great deal. He
and the younger brothers had gone to Russian schools. Then,
in the First World War, German troops had entered the town.
The older boys were taken to serve in the army; the younger ones
were formed into schoolboy regiments and marched eastwards to
dig trenches for German troops.

He was sixteen when the war was over. But for Poland it was
just beginning.

The two older brothers had families, but the younger ones had
already left, making their way westward, on foot and by troop
train, moving always westwards. Henri and Rudolf were already
safe, carrying with them, as my grandparents before them had also
carried, a bundle of linen which they would sell, and thus set
themselves up in business. Within a few days they were safe.
Safe where neither Russian nor Polish troops could reach them
now. They were safe over the German border.

But for my husband it had been too late. That year, 1919, he
was called up and sent for military training preparatory to serving
in Marshal Pilsudski's First Army of the Polish Republic. Next
year he was sent to fight the Bolsheviks inside Russia. Only a
remnant came back from the fighting near Kiev. Norbert was
among them; there had been many casualties in the fighting but
now there was something worse. Typhoid.

It was a killer in those days, and under those conditions. The
army hospital camps could not cope with the outbreak. His
brothers had found him near to death in a field hospital, and somehow had managed to smuggle him home hidden in a horse-drawn
cart. With their help the mother had nursed him, in a sort of

fever herself. He was her youngest, her baby. She knew she might never see him again, but she wouldn't let him die. For weeks afterwards he was too weak to be moved. She hid him in the flat in Lodz, above her little factory which made linen cloths.

To return to the army and the war against Russia meant a probable death, in his weakened condition. To desert, as so many were now doing, meant a certain death by shooting. Unless he could escape to safety over the German border. In Germany nobody cared any more about deserting Poles or Russians, or about fighting anybody.

There were so many dead Poles that it was a simple matter to get a false passport. It belonged to a dead friend, the son of a neighbour. It would be enough to get him on the train to Breslau, provided the border police did not examine it too closely. But it would be risky if troops boarded the train, looking for deserters.

His civilian clothes now hung loose on his wasted body. He put on a disguise, wore the black fur hat and grew long side whiskers like an Orthodox Jew. It was not until the train was close to the German border that the Polish soldiers came, combing the train from end to end, prodding under the seats, looking for deserters. But Norbert had not waited. He jumped. "All I remember of that time was the ferocious pain in my hand, which was somehow caught in the door of the train before I could get myself free."

Once in Germany, he was arrested immediately. "I sat there in the cell feeling happy."

All he had to do was to endure the pain in one badly injured finger, and to get a message to Rudolf, who was somewhere in Cologne, to come and rescue him. If Rudolf did not come the German police might decide to send him back, and he would be shot immediately.

Withing three days Rudolf had come, signed documents for his release, paid his costs, guaranteed his good conduct. Soon his hand was healing, he had a clean and comfortable lodging and a little job as wine salesman. Before long Rudolf and Henri had saved enough money to leave for Paris and set themselves up in a leather manufacturing business, west and still farther west, far away from the Russians and Poles. Rudolf and Henri even crossed the sea to visit an older brother named Will, who lived in Birmingham where he had been apprenticed as a boy. But England struck chill, and they returned to Paris to settle down.

I listened, only half understanding.

CHAPTER VI

MARRIAGE

I HAD NEVER expected to be as happy as this. I could hardly wait for him to come home from work each evening. Crouched at the window, I waited for him to appear at the far end of the green road.

There are some breeds of dogs who behave in that particular way when the master comes home at last. They streak to the door like a wild thing, they are beside themselves with joy; they leap upon the loved master to caress him without restraint. In a young wife it was unbecoming and unwise. I knew it was a rare husband who would enjoy it for any length of time.

At weekends we locked ourselves in our house and garden and pretended to be out. I had almost forgotten to worry, as always in the past, about my plainness. For I had a pretty figure, of which he quickly made me vain. On summer mornings I used to run laughing and naked through the house and garden, to gramophone extracts from Verdi and Puccini, while he gave chase.

Yet the habits of childhood were hard to break. I began to be uneasy. I had learned too long and too often to be wary.

Sometimes Father came to see us. Over dinner the two men discussed what was happening in Germany. Father said he could not believe the reports. The Germans, in his opinion, were a marvellous people. They were far too clever, too sophisticated, too independent-minded to be fooled by this funny fellow Hitler. Norbert said there was a lot in that. He thought Germany was marvellous too. He had always been happy in Elberfeld, and the people were mostly charming. But Germans just didn't like Jews and in the end it chilled you so much that you wanted to leave. There was nothing you could do about it; it was just something

c

unalterable that had to be accepted. Norbert switched on the radio so that we could hear the war news from Spain; it was the news from Spain, he said, that was really unbearable. Then they talked about Germany again as though Germany were some beautiful woman they had both loved and still adored after finding she was really a whore all the time.

Father looked tired and faded. He was going to see Abe and try and borrow some money, but he hadn't much hope. For a moment only I saw a glimpse of the old grin. He was seeing Mo too while he was in town. Afterwards I realised that it was the first time in my life he had mentioned the uncles without a quip or a joke, with none of the old acid. I was suddenly uneasy. I had, yes, everything in the world I wanted as we climbed the stairs, our arms round each other, to our cosy bedroom. It was a wild night, with the tall trees swaying outside so that long, loose branches waved appealingly in the lighted windows. I had kissed Father goodnight as he went out into the cold storm. There was another late night bulletin from Spain before we slept.

As the weeks went by, the uneasiness increased. Norbert was not well. It was chiefly due to worry. He had quarrelled with his brother, the one who had British nationality and had lived in Britain since boyhood. I thought of my fighting uncles and aunts who had also been born into different countries. Why did immigrant brothers have to fight and compete with each other? At least with the Russian relations it had all been comic, or Father had seen it that way. "Who threw Mo out of bed?" and Grandma, laying about her with the umbrella, and then turning on Grandpa in a fury because he refused to hit anybody. This was different, sad and bitter. The fighting Poles were not as funny even if they had all been born under the same Czar.

The worry was awful now. The business of Franklin Bros. (for Will had changed his name from Frenkel long ago) was liquidated, and we started on our own with a little factory, making gloves. But now we could only afford to employ half the number of people compared with the big leather-goods factory which the brothers had been running together. So Norbert's application for British nationality was turned down. It had been decided that he should apply to be put on the Polish list of applicants, though he had been born on Russian territory and carried German papers. But the Polish list was shorter, the Home Office said, compared with the Russian and German applicants, who were increasing every day.

One day two rather charming officials called from the Home Office. We were not to despair, they said, for if he could increase the size of his business and employ a large number of people then British citizenship would surely be granted in due course.

It became a race against time.

We decided to take our summer holiday in the Isle of Man. For it was too difficult now to get permission to travel without a passport. I determined to put my worries out of mind, and wrote gay letters to my eldest sister Beryl who, although only three years older than myself, had taken Mother's place in the family.

Father could no longer live in the town because he owed money which he would never be able to pay. He had taken refuge in Manchester with the three younger children, including my youngest sister 'Tina, who was eight. But he got on badly with my twin brothers, who had always been somewhat odd. They never liked him, and when they were eighteen they found a room to live in and went away.

But on a visit home Father was taken ill and went to hospital. Beryl and I went there one night when we learned that it was serious. Mo was there, walking up and down in a waiting-room. He said it was a crisis, and Izzy might not live through the night.

I pretended that I did not care. I even laughed, and said we had had so many crises. I didn't know why I behaved like that. In a way I was showing off in front of Mo. After all, he was almost a stranger. He and Father had fought each other all their lives, and it was hard to believe that he was worried now. It did cross my mind that perhaps he was sorry for everything but didn't know how to say so. I thought perhaps all the fighting all those years was unnecessary because the trouble simply was that they didn't know how to talk to each other. Just as I was not able to talk, naturally, to him now.

But I couldn't think of Father as dying or dead. He loved singing raucous songs about violent death.

> "And when we get to Newgate Street,
> Just to give the kids a treat,
> I'll show em where their Uncle Bill was 'ung."

Only a few months earlier we'd had a long talk together about everything. We had always found it easy to talk. We had talked about our Mother's early death and whether he felt it was all his fault, and he'd said he knew he was a bad husband. But it had been difficult to make her happy, he said, because from the start she'd kept asking if he really loved her.

He said he did love her always, but after a time he wanted to rebel. But he wished her alive, he missed her. And he said, "Even when I see your grandmother's grave, . . . I never liked her, you know that. But to be dead is the worst thing that can happen."

He also said that we should not blame him for having had so many mistresses and causing us all so much trouble. Sex, he said, was the thing that he had always wanted most. "It's the green in you, and when it stops then you are like a dry tree, brown and withered and ready to die."

He mentioned what had happened when Beryl, his first child, was born. It was the day King Edward VII visited our town, in July 1909. He loved processions and loud bands and royalty, and he couldn't tear himself away and go home and see if the young mother was all right and the first child safely born. When he got

home at last it was all over. But she never could forgive him
for it.

Mo was still talking, pacing the room, and we sat there, not
knowing what to say. When the doctor came and said there was
no change, we decided to go home.

Mo shouted at us, "I thought you were different from the rest
of our rotten family, but you're not."

Soon after leaving we got the news that Father was dead.

We didn't say much about it to each other. Except to discuss
'Tina, now a little orphan child, my youngest sister.

An orphan. It sounded like something from one of Father's
raucous, heartbreak rhymes or songs.

Beryl and Frank decided they would adopt her as their own.
She was rather a difficult child, who resented, as well she might,
having been deprived of her mother.

It was all a long time ago and many things have happened,
other deaths, other sorrows. I still think about Father, and miss
him almost every day.

It was a wild autumn, with heavy rain and high winds. We
stayed at home, which was cosy and pretty, except that every
evening there was news of more air raids over Spain, and often
there were live broadcasts of Hitler making speeches, and Norbert
used to translate them for all our friends.

Then the news broke about the future King Edward VIII and
Mrs Simpson, and we much preferred talking about that.

But Norbert was still not well, and had severe pain in hand,
arm and shoulder. The pain was now so bad that the doctor
suggested it must be a severe form of neuritis. A long session of
ultra-violet ray treatment in the local hospital outpatient department was arranged. But the pain got worse, much worse.

We were recommended to a more highly qualified doctor, who
examined Norbert and took quite a different view. It was not

neuritis at all; it was all due to red meat and drinking port. The patient must be put on a strict diet with medicine, and so on. Some weeks went by, and the pain was now continuous and more severe than ever.

The highly qualified doctor suggested that the kidneys might well be the cause of the condition, and suggested a kidney specialist. We travelled up to London to visit the best kidney man in Harley Street. He said he could not find anything wrong with the kidneys.

A nerve specialist was recommended and we went to see him, this time in the company of the doctor. After an examination, the verdict was pronounced. The patient was entirely healthy, and was suffering from an imaginary ailment and imagined pains. The doctor added his own verdict: "I am surprised," he said, "at a healthy young man imagining that he has all sorts of pains and symptoms. We can find no reason whatsoever for the mysterious pain."

When we got home I was for the first time uneasy and impatient with him. Was it possible that the quarrel with his brother, the worry of the past year, was making him neurotic? Perhaps because I was so much in love, I had let myself be fooled so that I did not see what the doctors saw. He could not touch his dinner. He crossed the room to get a pipe, and it struck me suddenly that he was much changed. He had been a big man; now he was gaunt and thin. He put a match to his pipe and smiled at me, the old, loving smile. I saw, in a flash, that he was going to die.

I got up and went into the kitchen, holding on to the sink tightly with both hands, trembling and shaking.

What utter rubbish. As though life could be so tragic, that it should end even before it began. I was letting the wariness painfully learned in childhood send me out of my mind.

I busied myself making a pot of tea and carried it back into the living-room. I was quite calm again, calm and cheerful; how foolish to let oneself be attacked by a sudden fit of depression.

It was one thing to see the truth quite clearly, and another to let myself believe it. Norbert was sitting by the roaring fire listening to the news from Berlin. In the commentary that followed, someone said that the situation looked serious but of course people must not think that it could lead to another war.

A neighbour said he thought my husband was not looking well. He would like to recommend a remarkably clever doctor who was attending his invalid daughter. The girl was now nearly twenty, and no doctor, no treatment, had been able to help her until now. "He is not like any other doctor you ever saw. Believe me, we have had a lifetime of doctors and we ought to know."

In the end I agreed that he should be asked to visit us. For one thing, he was a refugee from Hitler's Germany, from Berlin itself, and I knew that Norbert would be glad to have some first-hand news from there.

Dr Ilya Margolin seemed to fill our little hall. He looked, I thought, exactly like Father, only he was much taller and larger. Like Father he was very fair and white-skinned, with intense blue eyes and high cheekbones; a typical Russian.

"But I am a Russian," the doctor said, telling me his story as he followed me into the living-room. I felt the same excitement which Father had always brought with him into a room. The same intensity.

He seemed an odd sort of doctor. Instead of making an examination, as all the others had done, he just sat there looking big and pale and moon-faced, his blue eyes staring at us both, each in turn. Now and then he broke into German or Russian. "Nichevo—nye nado," he said when I offered a drink or tea or coffee. Something about his expression frightened me. If I read his look right, there was something about us that surprised him, something he had not expected to find.

As though reading my thoughts he suddenly said, "I was not

expecting to find such a nice young couple in this God-forsaken town where there is not a human soul for me to talk with."

Norbert laughed, but I was annoyed. Surely this, my home-town, was better than Berlin, where he had been a doctor on the staff of the University Charité Hospital until three years earlier?

Then the two men launched into a long conversation about Germany and what a wonderful country it was. The doctor said he had left Russia for Jena at nineteen to take his medical degree. Nothing more was said about the purpose of his visit to us.

But I was still worried. Something about us both had clearly shaken this doctor, and I could see that his kindly words of appreciation for us were certainly not the real reason. There was an ambiguous quality about him also. He sat very still, like some huge piece of the solid Russian land mass, so serene on the surface and underneath something boiled. When was he going to make his examination?

At one point he got up and went over to my husband, looking deeply into his eyes, using a tiny torch to do this.

Yes, he would have some tea after all.

He followed me into the kitchen. He wanted me to keep Norbert in bed for a whole fortnight. But first he would arrange a visit to a radiologist for an X-ray of his chest.

This was a surprise. No one had suggested making an X-ray.

The doctor shrugged. "This is England. The English are a wonderful people; I like them best of all my patients. They ask for nothing, expect nothing. And the doctors here . . . they know nothing and they do nothing. You must not tell anyone what I say, of course. Here they prefer the etiquette, nicht?" He had an attractive smile. "I do not know what is wrong," he said, "but in a fortnight I will tell you."

It was always one of the hardships of my life that when my feelings were strongly involved I could always hear quite clearly not only what was being said but also what was not spoken at all.

The doctor talked often about his brief married life. His wife, a clever doctor, had preferred women, including some of her patients.

"Yet I still loved her more than any other woman because, for one thing, she was the only one who bore my name."

She became a Communist and was taken prisoner in Spain. He only knew now that she was ill in prison there. He would give anything, do anything, to have her freed, but there was little hope. His letters, parcels, were all returned to him.

He did not greatly admire women. They did not, he said, usually behave well. Englishwomen were the best types; they behaved better than most. "To behave well; for me that is a way of life." He had a woman friend, a Scotswoman, who behaved well at all times. Ach, but she did not have a warm heart.

I realised that for him life would always be flawed in some important respect and that, in a way, this was how he preferred it. He could be involved, but never totally committed. He was saved by the flaw.

He did not approve of Mrs Simpson or Edward's love for her. "It is mad; at her age. Soon she will no longer be a woman. A woman must have children before she is twenty-four. Even twenty-four is late."

Sometimes he would turn our radio switch, trying to find some Russian station. For twenty-five years he had been away from Russia. Now in his middle-age he thought of nothing else, of the scenes and sounds of his childhood. Perhaps he should never have left. Perhaps that was his great mistake. He could have married some passionate Russian who would have understood him and his need for total love and devotion. Now it was too late to go back. So now he would never know. He would never find out if there too, at home in Russia, he would have found the same flaw that had destroyed Germany for him, that chilled him in England which he so loved and admired.

He moved his hand to the radio, trying to find a station. A voice was singing, "Wake up little fool, you never can win, I've got you under my skin."

He brought me the X-rays two weeks later, and two high-ranking specialists from London. They said there was no hope. It would last about ten months, perhaps a little less. They would try and prescribe for controlling the pain, but it would not be easy. The patient, they advised, should not be told the truth.

The doctor said little but behaved quietly, almost humbly in front of the specialists. After they had gone he stayed with me for a short while. He took me in his arms and muttered over and over in Russian how sorry he was. We were the only people he had found to like in England, and now he would have to suffer this long ordeal, perhaps ten months of it. So now he wished he had never met us. His arms, hands, shoulders were so strong and powerful; he was stroking my hair. I suddenly loathed him.

"Yes, strike me, hit me if you like. I tell you, we do not know what it is; nobody knows; even the specialists do not know, we know nothing."

Cancer of the lung was still rare in young men in 1936.

CHAPTER VII

THE END OF THE MARRIAGE

NORBERT WAS NOT handsome any more. The powerful figure dwindled rapidly, and his clothes hung loosely round him. He insisted on getting up each day, and sometimes he would start to make the journey to his office to try and work. He often got as far as the bus-stop and then returned, silent, defeated, to sit in the armchair by the fire, his right arm bent across the chest with the fist clenched over it as though to stem the wound within.

One night I turned back into the room, after staring out at the snow-white fields and between them the tall trees, their branches quite still under a load of glittering snow blossoms.

It was nearly time for another dose of morphine hydrochloride, and Norbert lay still under the sheets. He was so still, scarcely breathing. Only the thick silky black hair seemed alive against the pillow, and the blue and red flame of the gas-fire and the richer purple and scarlet of anemones in a bowl.

Suddenly I had a sense of exaltation at the strange beauty of the scene. I felt safe and peaceful as though all anxiety had left me.

I sat beside the bed until he woke and then, instead of pouring out the hated "medicine", I lay down beside him on the bed. I put my face close to his and began to whisper in his ear. "I was watching the gas-fire while you slept. Darling, I know it will be all right in the end, but I cannot watch the pain any more. I could turn that tap on us both, we should be together and safe."

He could not move because now the pain was strong again, but he turned his head and smiled.

"No," he said, "there is always time to die."

Twice in those ten months the pain suddenly, unaccountably,

stopped. I was measuring the morphine in a teaspoon, the dose he was allowed every few hours.

"Take it away," he said, "I don't want the vile stuff." His face was radiant.

"Get your coat," he said, "we're going out. We'll have tea, go to a theatre; we've not been out of the house for months. I will make it up to you."

We were quite lightheaded that afternoon, as though we were both a little drunk. The pain was gone. He could lift his useless arm and shave himself.

We bought theatre tickets, and in the restaurant first we laughed and talked about our plans for the future.

In the theatre nearly an hour later, sitting in the darkness, though he did not speak, I knew the pain had returned. I could not see his face in the darkness, but I knew how it would look if the light went up. Then he said, "Let's go."

Outside I ran in a frenzy for a taxi while he stood, waiting, not saying anything. The street lamps now glared down cruelly on his face. At home I flew upstairs for the bottle and spoon. He begged me to give him a little extra this time. Soon he lay in a deep sleep like a coma. I sat down by the fire and waited for him to wake.

After that we rarely left the house. Almost every day Dr Margolin came, bringing supplies of drugs. We tried heroin, Pyramidon and morphine in various forms.

We listened to all the news bulletins, the war in Spain and China, all Hitler's speeches, the news of King Edward's romance. Sometimes, in spite of the blazing fire, the scene inside our rooms was more and more ghostly, so that the shrieking voice of the Führer of the Third Reich was a link with outside.

Sometimes I got up in the night and sat at the bottom of the stairs and wept silently.

If the pain became more severe, I telephoned the doctor to

bring more morphine because an injection was more potent.

Norbert said, "First you must give the doctor a meal; he has been on his feet all day."

I said I would give him nothing until after the injection. The doctor laughed, "She cares nothing if I starve to death; she cares only that you are all right." He prepared his instruments, sighing. "I wish only that some woman just once in my life loved me in this way. But it never happened."

As the weeks went by, the chemist often refused to supply more morphine unless I had a fresh prescription for the day. If the doctor had been out all day on his rounds, I might not have enough left by the evening to last us through the long night.

Dr Margolin, tender as he was to us, was determined never to flout the letter of the law in the tiniest detail.

"I am foreigner," he said, "and no one shall say I will not be careful."

Our remaining money was dwindling fast, and the cost of the morphine was high. What would happen if there were no money left to buy it? . . .

One night, as he lay as though in a coma, for I had been obliged to increase the dose, there was a knock at the door which alarmed me, so late it was, and it was rare now for visitors to call. On the doorstep a man thrust an envelope into my hands. It was a lawyer's writ from Norbert's brother Will, demanding payment of £1,000 for alleged loss of business due to the earlier liquidation. For a long time I sat staring in an idiot way at it. Almost it was a kind of relief to hate someone as much as I hated Will then, because it was a brief distraction from the one thought beating in my brain, the one that never stopped.

So history was repeating itself, setting brother against brother again, again.

The second time the pain stopped, he sat up in bed and wanted to read something. He asked me to go to the village and buy him a magazine in which he knew a certain article was appearing about what was happening in Germany.

I ran out, almost happy for an instant. Surely this was a good sign. Surely the doctors were mistaken. It was not too late for a cure to be found.

When I got to the shop, they had sold out. It was nearly five o'clock. If I were quick, I might get a copy elsewhere. I ran wildly to the next shopping centre, not daring even to stop and wait for a bus.

But they had sold out too. They suggested I should try Five Ways, but when I got there, panting, the answer was the same. All copies sold.

Now I was almost in the town. I knew the big Smith's store would still be open, and they would be sure to have a copy. They were just closing as I stumbled in, too breathless to speak for a few moments. So sorry, there had been a big run on the magazine.

I stared back, unbelieving and then started to wander round the shop, distractedly picking up papers, magazines. It must be here. He asked for nothing day after day. It was only a little ninepenny paper that might for a few moments interrupt the nightmare.

They wanted to close the shop and put up the shutters. And I was in the way.

When the spring came the doctor insisted that we should go to the seaside. This was chiefly to keep up the fiction that he was getting better, that the treatment was doing him good. The deep ray treatment had been a failure, turning him from a sick man into a ghostly figure. The drugs were losing their effect, and injections and trials with new drugs were so varied and involved that I was able to pretend that this was some sort of "treatment".

In the first few days, however, I realised that the trip had been a mistake. The little seaside town was gaily decked with coloured lights and coronets for the coronation of King George VI. There were noisy parties at night. By day, the seaside visitors stared after us. Even now, tortured, he was an upright, romantic-looking figure with the ghostly remains of his dark good looks, the black silky hair.

We would hurry into the hotel, hoping to avoid the curious ladies in the lounge, but there they always were.

"And shall you go to London for the coronation ceremony?" said one.

"Don't you think he will make a very good King?" said another.

"That wicked, wicked woman," said a third, "but she has learned her lesson about the English character."

"And how are you feeling today?" they asked my husband. "I was only saying to my sister today, what a pity . . . such a nice young couple, such a pity you cannot get out more into the sunshine."

Upstairs, we giggled a little about the ladies. "I wish we had brought Margolin," Norbert said. "He would enjoy the company of well-behaved women."

Next day the pain sharpened suddenly, and one eyelid drooped constantly. In a panic I took him by taxi to the nearest doctor and asked him to wait while I told the doctor our story. My fear was terrible that he would now at last begin to suspect the truth because of having to leave him sitting there in the taxi. But it was clear that the pain was too much for him to consider this situation or to see there might be anything odd in it.

I was alarmed too when the doctor met Norbert. He was in his late twenties, a sunburned, pleasant young man with a lovely young wife, also a doctor, whom we met in the hall carrying their baby. They had only been in practice for a few months.

The doctor's hands were shaking as he examined my young husband, and the dismay on his face was unmistakable. But Norbert had not noticed. As always he was watching me, and I knew that it was only a sign of fear from me that would make him suspicious.

An immediate operation for injecting alcohol into the spine was arranged in a luxury nursing-home nearby. I did not even ask the price, knowing that it would be in any case far beyond what we could afford. I had never been good at taking decisions, but now it was getting easier, simply because there was no alternative one to be considered.

The operating theatre was all glaring light and heat. He made a sign for me to come near. I bent down to hear his whisper. He wanted to know how the X-rays had looked; were they any better? If so, swear it, by our love for each other.

I whispered back, so that the theatre-nurses could not hear, that they were better, much better, I swore it.

From this day, I started to collect some of the tablets from each phial and to hide them in my handbag. It had not been possible before in any case. But the young seaside doctor was quite different from Margolin. He insisted on my taking a prescription for two hundred tablets at a time. At first the local chemist refused to serve me, but I arranged for the doctor to speak to him about it. Now each night while Norbert slept I undid the phials and removed some of the tiny half or quarter grain tablets of morphine, heroin, Pyramidon or barbiturate.

When we got home, Margolin suggested that Norbert should go into hospital for a few days, where a surgeon would cut some of the nerves involved, so that the right arm and hand would have no sensation at all. He would be able to put his hand in the fire and feel nothing. It sounded almost too good to be true. But we did not ask why it had not been suggested before.

The operation was performed the following day, and Norbert died almost immediately afterwards.

Dr Margolin drove me from the hospital to Beryl's house, and on the journey he said he was glad that my husband was dead because now the dreadful pain was ended. He said there had been no hope ever from the beginning. He said I must not be angry with him because he had done his best all the time. And I said that was true, and we shook hands at the gate.

I was put to bed in Bettina's room, and my clothes were taken away, everything except my handbag which I kept hidden inside the bed.

Bettina brought me a cup of tea. She was now a pretty little girl of thirteen, and her face was very sad. I remembered that she had told me once that she was afraid to like anyone very much because they always died. She did not say anything, and I was glad because there was nothing to say. . . .

When it started to get dark, and I took the phials and tablets out of the handbag; I felt I was repeating something I had done weeks and months ago. I couldn't decide whether this was because I had dreamed it or rehearsed it in my mind. At the same time I felt divided. I was twenty-four, and I did not want to die. In spite of having had no food for several days, I felt enormously strong and healthy. I felt as though I could go running through the town and out into the country for miles without tiring. So it felt wrong when I started to swallow the tablets, not morally wrong but because of this, my extraordinary good health. I had this perfectly working machine, and now I was going to spoil it.

Then I realised that the machine was not perfect because my head was hurting terribly. Not with any kind of headache, but my thoughts were hurting it; they were hitting my head like blows from a stick.

I had several hundred tablets, including about a hundred half-grain morphine, and it would take too long to swallow them all. I dropped the lot in the remainder of the cold cup of tea and swilled it down. The taste was filthy.

I put all the empty phials and bits of broken glass back into my bag. It had been difficult, hands shaking, to remove the tiny tablets from the tight tubes, so I had cracked them open. One finger bled slightly, and I bound it up in a handkerchief so that it would not mark the sheet. I took the bag, with the two letters, one for Paris, which I had already written inside it, tightly into my arms and lay down under the bedclothes. My heart was knocking loudly in my ears. Then I slept.

I once wrote an account of the events that followed. Reading it through again after many years, I felt differently about it. There was nothing that I would change because it was all true, but at the time I wrote it I was still suffering from self-pity, and I think this showed. It was not just that I had stopped pitying myself, but more that later I began to think that pity is harmful, whether it is for ourselves or for other people.

CHAPTER VIII

THE DOCTOR

For I had reckoned without the doctor, or in fact given him a thought. I had reckoned without the strange, unreasoning fear of policemen and officials, of Home Office enquiries and medical board investigations, felt by Dr Ilya Margolin. I had reckoned without his passionate gratitude to the Britain which gave him refuge. This took an almost exaggerated form, though he liked to pretend a little comic resentment for the law which had sent him, at the age of nearly forty-five, to Edinburgh, to study all over again for his medical degree.

Like many who had lived in Germany he had an exaggerated respect for police of any rank or description, and for authority in any form. He was constitutionally unable to pass a uniformed policeman at a street crossing. He would slow down and sometimes stop the car. He would raise his hat or incline his head, the while bestowing upon an astonished policeman the broadest extent of his smile.

Parking the car was a major operation. For he would seek out every policeman within a radius of a quarter of a mile of the affected area, in order to satisfy himself that he had upon his side the full and willing permission of the law to leave his car for a few minutes unattended. Nor, having found the policeman, could he forbear to detain him for conversation, during which the doctor would treat each word that fell from the constable's lips as though, verily, this was not a conversation vouchsafed to ordinary mortals on an ordinary business day but a privileged audience with one of the uniformed masters of the realm.

That was Dr Margolin, faithful, intelligent, kindly, but almost hysterically anxious to keep always on the right side of that august, imperial body, the Home Office which had granted him a new life in a new country.

The story of how he reacted when he felt that august protection threatened was told to me later, partly by himself, partly by Beryl, so that I was able to piece together the events of the next five days, while I lay unconscious.

When Dr Margolin left Beryl's house that Sunday afternoon after the fatal operation he was anxious. The first hours of widowhood for the wife of the patient whom he had nursed so devotedly for a year (to send in a bill would have been, of course unthinkable) had been for him rather trying ones. The girl had been upset, naturally, hysterical even. Women—he thought of his long and complicated experience of them at the Université Charité Hospital in Berlin—were unpredictable.

Then Beryl telephoned next day about noon. Olga, she said, would not wake up, and her face and fingernails were turning black. Would he come as quickly as he could?

When he got into his car, with a vision now in front of him of a coroner's court, of policemen—much less respectful now, in his vivid imagination—of discreet enquiries from the Home Office, of gossip, he drove in a way that broke the habits of a lifetime. He did not stop at the traffic lights, nor look for indignant police constables. He drove as though something worse even than the Nazis were after him.

"As I drove, like a madman," he said afterwards, "I felt that all was crashing around me now, because of the hysterical act of a stupid girl."

Beryl said, "I opened the door not to a man but to a fiend. There were shouts in Russian and German, a tirade of oaths and curses."

They rocked the little semi-detached house in a quiet road. He did not wait to sterilise his instruments, but plunged strychnine into the dangling wrists of the body on the bed. He shouted for a stomach pump; he shouted for an ambulance. And, when it came, out stepped two solid figures in policemen's blue.

For the next four days, while I remained still unconscious at the hospital, Dr Margolin tried to concentrate on his work in the surgery at home. But finally he could wait no longer. On the fourth day he drove to the hospital and went inside the ward. Sister in the Dudley Road hospital, Birmingham, was pessimistic. As she had kept telling him on the telephone, there was no change.

"Oxygen should be tried," said the doctor. "In Germany I have seen cases like this come round even after a week."

"I take my orders from the doctor in charge of the hospital," said Sister, "and he is not here just now."

"Then bring Matron here," he said. "I intend to give oxygen." Sister did not move.

"Do you bring Matron," said the doctor, "or do I?"

When Matron came she said, "Doctor, I really cannot allow this; you cannot give orders in this hospital. I am in charge here in the absence of the Superintendent."

In the end Margolin won. Oxygen was given. The struggle back to life was my first experience of pain. Unknowing, for hours I fought my rescuers.

The nightmare weeks that followed in that long, hot summer of 1937 are clear to me in each detail, each sight and sound. I am glad that the law is now changed and that no one is punished any more for trying to commit suicide. But in those years before the war you were handed over to the police to be committed to a prison mental institution for observation.

I hope and believe that such places are more humane today than they were thirty years ago, and yet I do not feel quite confident about it. There is something grudging in the English character which has its counterpart in the Russian too. Both peoples have what I call this "minimum" quality. Perhaps, in primeval times, other peoples decorated their caves with animal skins for warmth or beauty. But I imagine the earliest English and Russians left their caves bare. For them, a minimum would always be enough. Think of the so-called British Restaurants which were opened during the war. Even a speck of parsley might have helped. Or some wild daisies in a jam jar.

That is what Erdington House, Birmingham, was like thirty years ago. In those days there was a minimum of everything that made life tolerable.

Even today I cannot think of it without a shudder.

CHAPTER IX

THE MADHOUSE

I FIRST REGAINED consciousness in the Dudley Road Hospital, which was at that time no great shakes either.

Dr Margolin was nowhere to be seen. By my bed sat a bearded Rabbi (who could have sent for him, I wondered?) intoning hymns for the dead and swaying back and forth in orthodox manner. He stopped, hesitantly, on seeing that the body on the bed appeared, suddenly, to be alive. Then he began again, as though slightly annoyed at the interruption.

Suddenly my bed seemed surrounded with faces. I was sobbing why had they not let me die? A white-coated Superintendent, grey-haired, thin and upright, regarded me from the end of the bed with some distaste.

Certainly it was not a pretty scene, resembling those second feature films or bad television scripts where the sinful girl is confronted by the good doctor and given occasion for several minutes of rousing dialogue.

"Disgusting," said the Superintendent. "Get her out of here. She has caused enough trouble in this hospital already. It is against the law anyway to keep her longer."

Two little nurses were scurrying about, removing bandages and lint from a deep wound on my thigh and wiping away the pus which poured from it. "The hot bottle!" It was clear they had not expected my revival any more than I had. A number of staff gathered round the bed to stare at the damaged face, criss-crossed with scratches, bloodstains and bruises. They looked at the blistered feet, also burned by the hot bottles, and at the bruises stretching the length of arms, legs and back.

I was wrapped in blankets and taken in a police van for a short journey. I did not know then that the nightmare was about to begin. There was even a kind of bitter peace in the acute pain and discomfort. For I could barely remember the reason for my condition. Again I was finding how some advantage could be wrenched from disaster.

The long, narrow ward was hot and airless, but at first I did not notice that the tall windows were practically closed in spite of the summer heat.

"Put it on the floor," I heard a voice say, "there is no bed ready yet." There was something in the woman's voice that I had never heard before.

Later I heard the voice again when I begged for water. It was difficult to make oneself heard, because for one thing my throat was so parched and painful that it was difficult even to whisper, and for another the ward was full of noise. I could not distinguish what the sounds were, though sometimes the noise rose to a piercing shriek.

It began to get dark, and since I was lying flat it was not possible to distinguish between the forms hurrying past my stretcher on the floor. "Here . . . you must help yourself now," said a nurse thrusting a hospital cup into my hand. I reached longingly for the water but the cup fell immediately from my nerveless hand, crashing in pieces on the floor, before I could take even one sip from the spout.

Suddenly there were two women in uniform on either side of me. "You wicked girl," shouted one, her voice harsh above the shouting in the ward. "You do that again if you dare," said the one on the other side. "Here, nurse," she called to someone, "keep your eye on this one. I hope she's not going to get vicious. Started throwing cups about already."

Another face approached, and the voice was gentler this time. I saw that the face was lined and weary. "Now behave yourself do," said the weary face, "or you'll get no more to drink today."

Later the ward became quieter; it was quite dark except for the lamp shining on the night-duty nurses. They lifted me into a bed, whispering together. Then they brought bowls and a catheter and pushed the tiny tube into my bladder. I could hear them talking . . . "tablets . . . poison . . . smashed cups."

They examined my various injuries. "You have made a mess of yourself," the Sister said, as she wrote something down on a record sheet.

Towards dawn, after that long, hot night, I saw a light switched on at one end of the ward. There came the sound of heavy boots and scuffling. Turning my head, I saw two policemen enter the ward dragging between them the struggling figure of a woman. The night nurses ran towards them, and there was no other sound but the heavy breathing of the little party locked in a strange, silent embrace. As though in some ghostly ballet, the figures twisted and writhed in the half-light, to the accompaniment of panting and an occasional long sigh.

It was soon over, and I listened to the men's heavy footsteps going down the stone steps. The struggling woman, who was now lying on a bed near the door at the end of the ward, was quite still.

Only when the bright light of early June filled the windows was I able, by twisting my head, to see that there were people all round me. There were people in the beds and others moving about in the narrow space between the two rows of beds on either side.

Suddenly I heard loud laughter and chuckling from the bed on my left. A girl of about seventeen was sitting up, wearing a coarse sack-like nightgown. She looked healthy and strong and her hair hung all round her, almost covering her face. In her hand was a roll of toilet paper, and she appeared to be excitedly unwinding this so that the paper was strewn all over the bed and on to the floor. Then she would stop this and jerk the paper towards her, and kneeling upright in her bed she bent low over the bits of paper, chuckling and murmuring. She appeared to be drawing or scribbling on the paper.

Suddenly a terrible cry rang through the ward. An old woman's voice was screaming: "'Arry, it's time to put the kettle on. 'Arry. Make the tea now, 'Arry, there's a good boy." The cries, which were repeated unceasingly for the next few hours, came from the bed opposite.

Someone was sitting on the end of my bed watching me. It was the figure of an elderly crone; grey hair straggled down, grey clothes hung on an emaciated form, her eyes stared vacantly but the grey lips smiled. In her hand was a broom and dustpan, a duster was over her shoulder.

"Don't she get on your bleeding nerves, that one," said the crone. "She's blind, that one. Blind as a bat she is. Thinks she's still at home, she does too. I get sick of hearing on that cupper tea. Can't get near her either, you can't. You hear her scream when the doctor comes."

I stared back at the woman, too frightened to open my parched, dry mouth. But she got up then and shuffled away down the ward, pushing the broom in front of her and making dabs with the duster at people and beds and walls.

By the time the doctor came to make his daily round, I knew by the cries coming from the beds on either side of me and from the bed opposite that these patients were out of their minds. The blind woman seemed to sense the presence of the doctor, and her screams raked the ward with fearful ugly, gasping shrieks.

The doctor stopped by my bed.

"Why am I here?" I said. My voice was hoarse but as steady as I could manage. "I am not mad," I said.

"Ah," said the doctor pleasantly, his rather plump face beamed down at mine with fond goodwill, "but you did a mad thing, don't you remember?"

"But you know I am not mad, you can see I am not mad," I repeated, and the words echoed strained and a little high-pitched in my ears.

"See how excited you are getting now," said the doctor. "That shows you are not in a normal state of mind. All insane people believe they are sane."

He bent closer, adding softly in a confidential tone, "All the people you see here believe they are quite sane just as you do."

In the next few weeks I knew that I was in constant danger of proving to the doctor that he was right. There never was a time, day or night but more especially at night, when the ward fell into quiet. Sometimes the grating, uncontrolled voices of the mad or the half-mad made quieter patients cry aloud in weary protest that only added to the row. I came to know each patient not by their names or illness but by the sounds they made, and often they were the fearful, animal noises of lost creatures.

By day many of them dressed themselves, or in their night-gowns walked or shuffled about, peering into other beds. I tried hard not to shrink or shudder when faces, vacant or menacing or silly, came close to mine. I was ashamed to show that I shrank from them. Was I now not one of them? For me, too, the windows were closed and barred against the hot June sun, except for a small locked opening at the top. I too had been deprived of my belong-ings to prevent any attempts at swallowing a morsel of wedding ring, comb or mirror. Looking at the anguished, grey and greasy faces round me I knew, without a mirror, how I looked now. And once I shouted out with fright when a fellow patient came close to me and tried to touch me, though she was no more than young Bettina's age.

It happened a few days later, about midday. The tin bowls full of some tasteless rice had already been taken away, with the spoons which the patients were given instead of knives and forks. My own diet was restricted to sips of water only, but I shuddered at the half-empty tin bowls full of the smell of washing-up water. The food was served by a little corps of women patients whose mania and frenzy had, it was said, long ago been cured. But they had never been given their freedom, and as this place was now their home they were bidden to share in the work of keeping it clean, which they did with a silent melancholy and listlessness more horrible to see even than the maddest patients who still had to be smacked or sedated or forcibly washed.

Suddenly a young girl dashed into the ward and the usual fight began, which was now almost a daily occurrence. Sometimes at night the policemen came to help control the struggling patients, but in the day-time a large staff of nurses were always ready to rush to each other's aid.

Now, in daylight, this young girl was too quick for them. Lithe and slim, she flashed from corner to corner, door to door of the long ward. Some of the walking cases rushed to guard the doors at each end to prevent her escape. While the fight lasted, they stood giggling at the girl's desperate struggles. There was no loyalty, I saw, among the insane. But the nurses could not hold her, and more came running. The girl was incredibly strong; now there were three, four, five, six nurses, including one male nurse, taking part in the wrestling, and all, except the girl, were spent and breathless.

The figure twisted, turned, panted, now close to my bed. The girl's clothing was hanging in strips about her, and the white aprons of the nurses were torn. Slim and white, she was a swinging maypole, and the torn uniforms flying around her in a frenzied dance were its fluttering white ribbons.

The face of the crazed girl was startlingly pretty. She was perhaps fifteen, with yellow curls and a flawless, pale complexion which was particularly striking among the blotched red and purple faces of the sweating nurses. The girl had violet eyes, fringed in thick black lashes, and her features had a chiselled perfection.

She became, after a long while, exhausted. The band of nurses laid her on a bed and two of them sat upon her still wildly threshing limbs. For once the ward was quiet, as though sated with the enjoyment of this performance. I watched as she lay there, how her body jerked and quivered like some giant fish that continues to leap and spring in the net long after it has been snatched from the water.

Next day I was moved into a tiny partition at the end of the ward. It was just a cubicle. Suddenly, there she was, standing framed in the opening of the cubicle which had no door. It was the beautiful girl of yesterday's struggle, still wearing her old brown dress, which had been roughly stitched together so that it clung tightly to her young limbs.

We both stared, frozen, transfixed at the transformation in each other. For I had at last been washed and combed by Beryl, and dressed in her best bed-jacket. And this girl's beauty was gone. The chiselled features were blurred as though a blow across the face had turned its outline into a caricature of yesterday. The yellow curls hung matted, a greasy brown about her neck. The perfect lips hung open, the tongue lolling between the white teeth, as she came stumbling, lurching towards me, leering.

"Nice lady," she said in a thick voice, and put out a hand to touch my hair.

I thought I screamed, but no one seemed to hear above the clatter of the ward.

The girl made another lurching move, and this time I cried out, covering my face with my hands.

A nurse came running, then stopped, grinning and watching to see what the girl would do. I was afraid of them both.

"Nice lady," said the girl again and this time the nurse caught her hands as she bent over me.

"She won't hurt you," said the nurse, "she's all right now, aren't you, ducks? It's safer to take her round the wards with us than to leave her in the children's ward. Poor kid."

I was surprised. It was the first time I had heard a kindly word said for one of the patients. All day long the nurses were scolding, shouting, smacking, running. I knew it was not their fault, but it had left its mark, and it was a shock to see that they could be gentle also.

The girl's mania had come with the onset of menstruation. And only a few beds away lay a woman who had once been a teacher and had gone off her head with the menopause. She was one of the worst cases, in the nurses' opinion, fouling her bed and sometimes trying to smash the window and throw herself out. She was the one who got the most smacks, and I could hear her weeping sometimes. It was dreadful when she sang. "Jesus, hold me, Je-sus." Sometimes her husband came to visit, and I saw him walk, wanly, by. She was kept now in a high cot, like a child.

It seemed now as though I had not had any other life but this. As though there were no other life outside.

Outside, though I did not know it, in the fierce July heat beating down on that great prison yard and the mean streets beyond, a fight was going on to save me. Beryl, my eldest sister, the once languid beauty of whom our parents had been both proud and nervous, my aloof, detached sister, was fighting a lone battle to get me out. There were almost daily meetings with the hospital doctor, who, according to the law, had absolute rights over every patient put into his care.

He did not like suicides. "They always try it again," he told Beryl.

She was visiting local councillors, protesting, pleading. But it was no use. And the weeks went by. I neither ate nor slept, but shrank down under the coarse sheet, trying to shut out the sounds, the animal groans and cries. I was afraid, very much afraid. The law in those days was strict. If it had not been for Beryl's prolonged struggle to save me, I suppose I too might still be in that place, pushing my broom, flapping my duster uselessly against the iron beds. Not many people, I was told, ever were released. For who was there to come and fight and claim them back?

But luckily for me there was Beryl, and her brilliant idea to appeal to my rescuer, Dr Ilya Margolin of Hall Green, Birmingham.

All this time he had stayed away in order to punish me. He could not easily or soon forgive the injury I had very nearly caused him by putting in doubt, according to his view, his careful and impeccable professional behaviour. I had not behaved well. It repelled him and, knowing him, I understood.

One day, dazed with weakness and heat and noise, I lay there, despairing, concentrating fiercely on not hearing, not listening to the sounds of the ward. Then I looked up and saw him sitting at the end of my bed, watching me.

He was an emotional man, in his Russian way. Tears in his eyes, he forgave me. He promised that rescue was near. He had a plan. "I do it for your lovely sister," he said, "not for you."

After he had gone there were terrible screams from the blind woman who was being removed, now finally certified, to the insane asylum. All the occupants of the ward joined in, and a hideous wailing rose and howled throughout the building and beat against the closed, hot, dusty windows and echoed back and forth, as the mad and the half-mad clanged their tin bowls together until the noise was no longer itself but more a battle-cry of the benighted.

Dr Margolin saved me by a trick. Despite his almost servile respect for authority, he enjoyed outwitting his fellow doctors if he saw a chance. I had begun to cough blood, and the hospital doctor suspected that the results of my mad action were showing themselves in a rapid consumption. Dr Margolin, who knew this could not be true, confirmed this opinion . . . and, worse, suggested that I had now not long to live. He knew that it would be embarrassing for the hospital, without any facilities for treating a serious illness, to be faced with this prospect. The upshot was that Erdington House was only too happy to be rid of me and the tuberculosis with which, they believed and Dr Margolin confirmed, I was now threatened. He and Beryl signed the necessary documents accepting responsibility. I was free to leave. I could not believe in my happiness. Yes, happiness. I did not deserve it and had not expected it . . . to go out alive and free from that place.

He said that now I weighed no more than a child, as he lifted me, wrapped in a blanket, and carried me past my nearest neighbour in the ward. I did not dare to look at her as we pushed past her bed. Her silence was more terrible than any cry, for she was paralysed and had lain there for ten years. She was covered in bed sores.

At her home, Beryl put me in her own bed for the next six weeks.

The doctor came each day. Perhaps I should never regain normal health, but I could rely upon his efforts, he said.

I was grateful to him, and concentrated upon thinking about him only. His was no conventional method of medicine. He liked to slip my nightdress down and caress me, sometimes remarking in disgust, "Ach, so thin, now you have no figure any more."

Soon it was being said in the town that of course he, the lone refugee doctor and gallant hero of my story, would marry me. It seemed to many people a comfortable end to a slightly disgraceful story. Sometimes, sitting on my bed, he would repeat the rumours to me himself, now with a rueful satisfaction, because I was 24 and he was 47; and then more often with gloom.

"I do not want to marry," he said. "I had one experience. It is not for me. Besides, I liked you once, I do not really like you any more."

It was true. For one thing, I had behaved badly, the worst crime in his eyes. For another, I now had a flaw more fatal still. Just as he had been disappointed in Germany, then in England ("the lack of heart, of real warmth"), now he was disappointed in me. For whereas I had once been the devoted wife of another man, now I was not; which meant that my now available attractions were for him considerably reduced.

He began to find ever new failures in me, while the caresses continued along with his devoted nursing. One day he arrived to tell me of disturbing news he'd received about me from the wife of a former neighbour of the "Poor Davises". This was that our family history was turbulent, our late father irresponsible, our debts catastrophic, our behaviour immoderate, and, last but not least, there were twin sons who had some neurotic disorder. He was referring, of course, to my unhappy brothers. Even the crazed and wicked uncle who had shut his wooden door on the Izvozchik children all those years ago was included in the neighbour's story.

"So you see, a marriage is out of the question," the doctor said. "It is true I am lonely, but I cannot take risks. Already you have shown yourself quite unstable, and soon you will be twenty-five. It is too old to have a child."

As long as he stayed in the room, talking, I was content. It gave me something to think about in the long days of that endless summer. Besides, he looked in his fair, blue-eyed, snub-nosed Russian way, as Beryl also remarked, exactly like our Father. He was very much attracted by the enigmatic Beryl and her selfless care for me. I watched how, each time she approached the bed, he attempted to clutch and embrace her as she slid away as tactfully as possible. "You see," said the doctor in triumph, "our patient is jealous of my admiration for *you*."

D

To which she remarked that, if so, it was a good sign that her mad sister was on the mend and therefore she would not, as she often threatened, have to send me back "to that place".

It was true. I shut out the past which made my days peaceful and my nights terrible, with recurring dreams in which I played the part of a terrified Eurydice descending into the dark. But the very difficulties of my present illness, the result of a bronchiectasis and my other injuries, were enough to fill each day. And I continued, quite conscientiously, to think about the doctor. He was a provoking man, but he still seemed to be a likely solution to my problem. He was attractive. He had befriended me, and in the past eighteen months I had come to lean on him for help and advice almost every day.

My problem was simply that now I had no home, no belongings, no money, no job, no future. I could not continue to live on my sister and brother-in-law, whose own marriage had barely begun. They already had Bettina, our youngest sister, to rear and educate. Everything, even my clothing, had been sold to pay our debts, for the drugs and X-rays, and the business which had run to a standstill. The only one who had so far not sent a bill was the doctor himself.

The summer turned into autumn. I was able to get up and look at myself in the mirror. For the first time in my life I admired my looks. Such a gaunt, wasted face and figure; pale, pale as I had never been. Emily Brontë must have looked something like this before she died, I thought with satisfaction. Emily had the same long nose.

My younger sister Cora came in one day to show me something in the local paper. She was fond, but brisk and cheerful. I admired her; for one thing she seemed free of self-pity, in sharp contrast to myself, who felt that sometimes I was devoured by it. She had met a charming young man, and hoped soon to be married. I wondered why our mother had fretted so much about our chances. Getting married had once seemed to be such a far-off goal, such an impossible feat. Now my two years of married life were over.

Cora showed me an advertisement in the paper. Just as Father used to do. It was by a firm called Birmid Industries, who were opening a big new rolling-mill in the country a few miles out of town. They needed a German interpreter.

Life was repeating itself, putting me back again among the Germans and their electric ovens in which the metal alloys were cooked like cakes and pies.

Ah, I did not want to go back into the factory, the stink and heat of the foundry.

Beryl said, "It's up to you. If you really try hard enough, you could still get into journalism or become a writer and write that book as Father wanted you to do."

"What shall I write about?" I said. And there was no answer.

CHAPTER X

THE RECOVERY

FIRST REACTIONS AFTER a long illness are of pleasure in moving about. I enjoyed the factory sirens in the cold, early dark. Beryl insisted on my taking a tin basin of lamb and vegetable stew to work. She prepared it each day, and the house was now always filled with its poignant aroma. And when the tormenting fragrance rose in the freezing unfinished factory, its great walls wide open to the winds and snow blowing across the fields, the workmen came with wondering faces to sniff at where our office door should have been, if we'd only had a door. The typists let me heat the tin basin in their kettle. These were the same warm-hearted, affectionate girls I remembered from the old days. We had no heat, and only unfinished equipment. But one thing we did have was Germans, dozens of them swarming in their blue dungarees all over the foundry and laboratory floors. They came from Leverkusen-Schlebusch, from Berlin, Frankfurt, Cologne, from all over.

Life settled into a calm routine. Once again I saw the advantages of being poor. My wages were £3 10s. a week, so if ever I was to have a home again, or even just a room of my own, it was going to take some effort. I slept in the same room with my schoolgirl sister Bettina, and the long journey to work meant starting early and returning late, for there was no bus service in those days, and a long walk across the fields and lanes from the terminus.

If you do not like your life, you will take more interest in other people's to avoid thinking about your own. I had never been a good listener unless Father was doing the talking. Now, for the first time, I listened and heard what was said. Sometimes, on the early morning walk to the factory, a car would stop and one of the chief engineers would tell me about his life, his wife, his children. How extraordinary. Other people had problems too.

The German "Monteure" (Erectors) talked to me all day. About how unfair the Allies had been to Germany after the war ended in 1918. No, of course there would never be another war. Herr Hitler would see to that. Many people didn't like him, despised him even, but look what he had done for Germany. Everyone now had a job. Only they wished their job was at home. Here in England there was nothing for them. No theatres, no good restaurants where they could spend their money, so there was not much incentive to try and learn some English. I said I hoped they would not try, as that would put me out of a job. As the great extrusion presses and rolling mills were slowly assembled, my job was to translate the instructions on their blueprints and to interpret when the English workmen wanted the new machinery explained.

It was chilling now to read in the newspapers the constant word "re-armament", and to hear the Germans talk about all the factories in Germany which were already electrically-operated. How were we going to re-arm anyway, when we appeared to be years behind the Germans in our methods of manufacture for things like aircraft bodies?

Some of their chief engineers were officials of the Nazi Party. Nevertheless, it was a shock when Herr Dipl. Ing. Weisse, one of our Associate Directors, arrived one day to supervise the work. A tall, elegant, blond, the Herr Dipl. Ingenieur wore the regulation brown uniform of a high-ranking officer of the Nazi Party. He wore top-boots and carried a dog whip as he toured the plant, and, it was rumoured among the shop stewards, had been seen to give the Hitler salute on entering the boardroom. One day there was a big trade union meeting to discuss the situation. A resolution was passed to inform the Board of Directors that it would be a good idea for them to persuade Mr Weisse to change his clothes, to avoid the possibility of a strike among certain unions. The upshot was that the brown uniform, the boots and the whip remained, but in future his visits were confined to the inner offices and he did not appear upon the factory floor. The "Monteure" were astonished when I explained to them that there had nearly been a strike. "A Quatsch, a Quatsch (nonsense)," they said, and laughed and laughed. They also pointed out that their own foreman, who sported a voluminous mackintosh and trilby hat in a sort of caricature of an Englishman, held much higher rank in the Nazi Party than Herr Weisse. Clearly, he realised he didn't have the figure for it, though Weisse had.

Only my nights, filled with dreams that were not only terrible and horrifying but also, in some strange way, sinister and menacing too, and my weekends were now a problem. The dreams I could not stop, but for the weekends I now brought home extra work in the form of more blueprints and German specifications to translate. It meant hours of work with the help of technical dictionaries to earn as much as a pound or two, but it made the time pass.

On Thursdays I visited the doctor on his half-day, returning sometimes tearful, sometimes elated, but nearly always bewildered. He found me changed, he said. He did not like a woman who told coarse jokes, who answered back, who argued. Clearly my work with these Nazis at the factory was having its degrading effect.

But quite suddenly, one day, the Nazis simply disappeared. Gone. I arrived for work to find the factory at a standstill. The Germans were in Austria. Our workmen had been recalled to Germany on Hitler's own instructions.

Now the spring rains ran in below the factory doors and the great pieces of machinery lay about, unused, rusting in the damp air. There was nothing for it but to start dismantling some machines, re-design and copy spare parts, and try to get the factory going without them.

For me it was disaster. I was out of a job, a thing I'd dreaded all along. For I did not want time to think.

But the crisis was soon over to the Führer's satisfaction, and about half the men returned, announcing that the others were needed for essential work at home.

Still I was shaken, restless. I asked Beryl if she would mind if I went to look for work in London. After all, she was, in law, still responsible for me. She said simply, "I think it is a good idea."

I gave in my notice, and then I went to Dr Margolin to break the news that I was leaving, and to say goodbye. He was annoyed. He was against my going. Though some of what he said was brutal, it was also strictly true. He said that London was a terrible place for a girl on her own, without money or friends. I should find it impossible to get a job. "Your German and French are not good enough, compared with the refugee girls who are willing to work for almost nothing in order to be allowed to stay in England. Besides, you are provincial, you are not sophisticated, you are not well-dressed enough and not good-looking enough."

I laughed, though I did not feel like laughing. Who wanted the truth, least of all from your doctor, who was likely to be right, especially if he were just a teeny bit fond of you. But only a teeny bit.

"You can laugh, but I am speaking truth. No girl can survive in London without a protector. And you will not get a protector because you are not pretty enough. To me you look not too bad, but to them, no; it is not what they want. They want something blonde and . . . like this," he made a gesture. "You know what I mean, you are now too thin and you look Jewish too, because your nose is too long."

I said, really to keep my end up because I felt like crying, and I didn't want to go home again with a tear-stained face, "You sound, my dear doctor, like my Nazi friends at the factory. Except that one of the top Nazis there is terribly sweet on me; he told me that while he is in England he feels free to have a nice girl friend, and he specially likes Jewish ones."

"I knew it," said the doctor. "You have become coarse, vulgar. You were not like this before."

I protested that I was joking; that of course I had nothing to do with Nazis. His flaw, alas, was no sense of humour. He said I should go then, that I should regret it, that I should come running back to him. Then he put his arms round me and made love to me. And I cried after all.

I packed my small bag, took my last twenty pounds out of the Municipal Bank. The family were on holiday, so I locked the house and went to New Street station.

Though only 110 miles distant from my home-town, London in 1938, as the doctor had said, was a world away for a provincial widow of twenty-five, reared inside a family group so large that it mattered nothing that one half didn't speak to the other.

CHAPTER XI

TO LONDON

AUNT PHOEBE AND her two daughters had already made this move a decade earlier. Father had once visited them in Grove End Gardens, and caught the two girls fighting over a coat which one had borrowed without the other's permission. Father had been thrilled. It was the Izvozchik children all over again. They had torn each other's hair, and Father even thought it worthwhile to rush in and get his own face scratched so that he could come home to us to show the mark before it faded. We six in our home had always been a bit too tame for Father, and he seemed to think this girlish show of spirit quite inspiring, especially in the daughters of his best-hated sister Phoebe.

But I remembered the story and hesitated to make the first approach. They were ten and twelve years older, established, with their own friends, their own home, and, though they might possibly enjoy feeling sorry for me, they could not fail to envy me too, for having, for however short a time, achieved the married state they still hoped to attain. So I waited, wondering what to do as I trudged the dusty, hot streets of Holborn in that August.

Girls in those days were not sophisticated. I had no idea how to start. Finding a room, talking to a possible landlady, was something quite beyond me. For weeks I lived in a tiny cell-like room in the old Royal Hotel because the price was 5/9 a night for bed and breakfast, and by spending no more than a couple of shillings a day, on cheese rolls or poached eggs on toast, I calculated that my money would last until I found a job.

That summer was a bad time to look for work. What good was it to offer German and French shorthand in a city that had suddenly filled up with refugees from the Continent?

I was hungry and unemployed like many thousands of other girls. I met some of them, as we stood in long, long queues on the staircases of City offices waiting for an interview advertised but filled long before our turn could come. I was hungry and worried, and once again I realised what a help that was. It gave me something to think about. If you had no job and no money, then you knew that getting one and spending five shillings on a meal would seem almost like happiness.

Business in that hot summer of 1938 was very bad, and all the secretarial agencies had lowered their terms. The highest wage offered was £4 a week for private secretary, smart, attractive, with personality, etc. Advertisements like this always brought several hundred girls along hoping for an interview.

At the Fenchurch Street bureau I was interviewed by a young man named Mr Alabaster. I had waited all day in his outer office, following a call for "smart, attractive" personalities, and he was limp with exhaustion when my turn came.

"Sorry, Miss," he said. "Don't know where they all come from. Most of that lot have already got a job, but they go mad at the idea of getting £4 a week."

Next day I went without hope to the Lester Employment Bureau, which had also advertised a job at £4 a week. The job must have been filled, I thought, because it was already 10 o'clock when I got there, after being turned down at two other places.

Instead, I found one solitary girl sitting forlornly in the outer-room, waiting for an interview. She explained that several hundred girls had been there, applying for the job. Until a man came out and informed them that the agency's terms were 10% on the first year's salary, that is, about £11 to be paid in full immediately. A stampede followed, with all the girls rushing to get out of that place. I went away, because I did not have £11 either.

I was losing hope now. Perhaps after all I should have been better off staying at home, working for the Herr Dipl. Ing. Weisse, strutting about the foundry in his brown uniform and top-boots, whip in hand.

It was lucky that the weather was so hot that cups of tea and cheese rolls were more than enough to live on.

At night I typed out letters and applications for jobs in the way that Father had trained me to do. By day I walked down by the river, through the City and back, and sat on stairs with the other applicants for jobs. From eight o'clock in the morning we sat there studying the Situations Vacant columns in the papers, or munching a bread roll or listening to the barrel-organs playing "Any umbrellas, any umbrellas to mend today" or "One day my prince will come" from *Snow White and the Seven Dwarfs*.

Once I got a job, only to lose it in two days. My German grammar was not good enough, the man said, and he didn't like my personality much either. I shed a few tears, put on my black straw hat and was halfway through the door when he suddenly ran after me, seized me by the arm and started shouting in German. He said I must sit down at the typewriter again and write and sign a letter saying that I had resigned of my own free will. Frightened of his insistence and not understanding, I did what he said, and went.

My confidence was shaken. So the doctor had been right after all. Except that he had thought me not pretty enough to find a protector, whereas the man who had just sacked me had made me an offer.

I received other offers, too, sitting on park benches in St James's Park, watching the ducks and talking about life with others of the unemployed. Some had been without work so long, they had even given up looking for it. I often saw them later in the day standing on a soap-box in Hyde Park and telling the crowd about Mussolini and Spain and Hitler and India and all. I stood and listened to them for hours. It was something to do; it was nearly as good as having someone to talk to. Often at night, a crowd would gather in Whitehall shouting "Arms for Spain" or "Arms for China", and I would run excitedly along with them, no longer alone, caught up in a great running, seething mass of people. Until the mounted police came up from Scotland Yard and round and round the Cenotaph we ran, dodging the swinging truncheons. Now I was no longer alone.

One day I even found the courage to telephone the only other person whose name I knew. This was our Aunt Sally, youngest of Father's family. But he hadn't liked her either any more than any of the others so I had only met her once.

Sally had taken to spiritualism on being widowed. She was kind and calm, unlike all the other aunts and uncles. So I was found a little room in a crumbling old block of flats, and was taken, for the first time, to séances and spiritualist meetings near Victoria. There was always a large crowd, and they looked all faintly bemused and strangely contented in spite of the meagre messages they were given from loved ones on the Other Side. So this, then, was yet another way of spending the time. It seemed that I was learning quickly about all the possibilities that were open to me.

I could still count on earning between one and two pounds a week from a foundry in Birmingham which was installing German electrical equipment, and every few days an envelope arrived with specifications and blueprints to put into as good a technical English as I could manage. So I walked the streets and parks by day, and at night on Father's old German typewriter I did the translations. I also tried the papers again. Walking up and down Fleet Street, staring at the big newspaper buildings, I thought of Father dictating to me his long, strange stories of crime and adventure and love, and then sending them off to the papers. And of his surprise when they came back, as they always did. And of his belief that one day somehow they would print my stories, and so he hadn't minded so much all the disappointment.

And I thought perhaps there was something wrong about Father's stories, and I wondered what it could be. I ached to have him there to talk it over. Now I thought more about him than about that other one whose name I never said, now, even to myself. And it was such a relief to have something else to cry about, so I did sometimes, into the rickety old Adler machine which certainly needed a wash anyway. And then I imagined some of the editors writing back and asking me to call and see them to discuss giving me a job as a reporter, and I cheered up, thinking about that. It never even entered my head that this was not the way to become a reporter; not then and not now, in fact, not ever.

I just slogged away, a letter to all the national dailies and evenings, then the Sundays, then the agencies, magazines and journals, and then started on the provincials.

There were far more publications then than there are now. It wasn't that business was better, but that people had more time for reading, for there were several million unemployed as well as me, and in those days it was a luxury to own a radio. I didn't have a radio, but I used to listen to the news outside my landlady's door while waiting for her only son Cyril to come out of the bathroom.

It was a relief to get work at last after seven weeks of trudging about the agencies, but it seemed odd that I should get it when hope and money were all gone, as though life started to improve long after one stopped expecting it to do so.

It was a firm called Metal Supplies Ltd, and most of the staff were German. For the first time in almost two months there were people to talk to, and I was so pleased to have an office and people

I belonged to that I was the first to arrive in the mornings, except for Herr Berlinger.

It was little Herr Berlinger, about five foot high with fair curls growing vertically on his head, who had engaged me. He had large round blue eyes, like a child. He ran from one office to the other, beating his clenched fists in the air, crying, "I have been cut up" because the telephone lines from Berlin or Cologne or Amsterdam had gone dead while he was buying or selling some copper or brass or zinc at rock-bottom prices against a first-class letter-of-credit on the international metal market.

I was terrified my German would not stand up to his high-speed dictation, but Fraülein Behrend croaked in her guttural English, "Silly girl, I will help you." The beautiful redhead Fraülein Pinkas, who had just qualified as a judge in Berlin before fleeing to London, did all the difficult sums involving compound fractions in Reichsmarks and dollars and gulden and zloty. They amazed me. I had never known such clever girls. Just as once long ago at school I had been one of the favourites on account of my foreign origin, now I was everybody's pet because I was British. Life did seem odd and terribly unfair.

"A-Nichts, a-Quatsch," said Herr Berlinger kindly as he corrected my mistakes in grammar. "Not to worry. You type it out again before Herr Süss shall see it. I tell Herr Süss you are nice real English lady, and he is happy you come to us."

I groaned that someone ought to point out to little Herr Berlinger and the terrifying Herr Doktor Erich Mayer and the other Director Herr Paul Friedmann that I was no more "an English lady" than they were.

"Leave it as it is," said Fraülein Behrend. "If they think you are English you will be able to finish at six, whereas we have to go on till seven and later."

Meanwhile the long telephone calls to Germany became even longer and more intense. Sometimes they talked business and sometimes about what was happening over there. I was puzzled to hear Herr Berlinger talking so affectionately to Berlin and Cologne. Aren't they Nazis too, I asked him? The big baby blue eyes opened wide, wide and, little Berlinger chuckled. "Of course, *sicher* they are Nazis; poor Villi and Heinrich. I am with Villi like this"—he clapped his little fat hands together. "All our lives from school on, like brothers."

It was all very puzzling. The papers were full of news reports from Germany.

It was a very pretty blonde girl who worked the telephone in Metal Supplies Ltd., formerly Firma Süss & Friedmann G.m.b.H. of Berlin and Cologne, a girl name Iris Campbell, who said to me, "You ought to be in newspapers."

Iris had noticed I was becoming a fanatical newspaper reader. Our office, during that time of the Munich crisis, was on the third floor of Australia House, and I was always up at the windows to see what the newsmen had chalked up on their boards to sell the *Star*, *News* and *Standard*. Nearly every few hours now there was something new or terrible, and we were all restless and excited. I would run and buy almost every edition. And Iris, a sensible Scots girl, was shocked at all this expenditure.

Then, suddenly, it was all over. I was watching through the window on the Aldwych side, and I saw the message go up, in big black letters. "Czech envoy weeps."

And it struck me then—I think for the first time—that the best kind of writing might be the newspaper kind, short, snappy, staccato headlines. Nothing else was needed except those three words. Life was never going to be the same for any of us after that, because a Czech envoy had wept. And I made up my mind there and then that I was going to learn how to write like that. So that three words were enough to tell a story—much better than three hundred could do.

I began going at night to sit in the gallery at the House of

Commons. On winter nights it was the warmest place I knew, and it enabled me to save many shillings for the gas-meter. My visits there were mentioned to my own boss, Herr Doktor Mayer, who was the office bully and of whom I was very frightened. "Her German is terrible," I heard him say. "It is all Berlinger's fault"— he was jealous of his colleague, always watchful, and hopeful he would find him out in some mistake—"English lady she is not either, and not worth the £4 we pay her."

It was all strictly accurate, for the Herr Doktor, a highly qualified metallurgical chemist and a great pedant, was always accurate and exact in all his judgments, which, though they sounded spiteful, were just and fair. Once, in sheer terror of the sack, I went to the lavatory and locked myself in for a long time. I could hear him striding the corridor shouting, 'Where is Mrs Franklin, is she gone to Parliament?"

And so the spring came that year. And with it my old restlessness. I felt envious of Herr Friedmann, who had gone abroad on a long journey. I watched the pale, sweet face of Fraülein Behrend. I knew that she lived in great poverty, caring for elderly relatives on her earnings. Some women like her seemed to me so full of patience and kindness, as though they had no room for any other kind of feelings. At lunchtime I caught sight of Herr Doktor Mayer, coated and hatted, gliding downwards in the lift to the pillared hall of Australia House. With both hands he was holding to his mouth, which was moving grotesquely, two large square sheets of Rakusen's motzas. The motzas lay sandwich-wise one upon the other, and from each end protruded two slender pink tongues of salt beef. It was the Herr Doktor himself, celebrating the Passover with all due ceremony. As the lift sank below floor level I caught, silhouetted against a shower of motza crumbs, a glimpse of the astonished lift-girl's face.

I felt that Metal Supplies was my whole life now, and missed it during the lonely, silent weekends. One Saturday afternoon I walked in Hyde Park to look at the guns. I watched as two balloons, bright silver, sailed in a rain-grey sky. Lower and lower they came, like the heads of great elephants with their trunks curled round their heads.

Elderly ladies squealed in fright. It was difficult to convince them that there was no one in the balloons. As the silvery mass collapsed upon the grass, the crowds surged forward to investigate the prostrated body. Trim nurses demonstrated first-aid, sirens hooted, and ambulances dashed backwards and forwards. When the first guns went off, I jumped several feet in the air, heart pounding. I soon became accustomed, however, and marched about bravely. Tin-helmeted soldiers perched and pirouetted on the tops of tanks and armoured cars and wise-cracked to the admiring crowds milling around them. A large white tent for the recruiting of new members for the Territorial Army stood invitingly open.

As dusk fell a drizzling rain set in, but the crowds remained. Parents wandered about, and in their wake followed eager, interested children. Soon it was quite dark, and the search-lights, operated by soldiers in khaki and tin-helmets and cordoned off in a great space, threw an eerie light over the park. The lights were swivelled, hunting the sky. Someone screamed. The rain fell faster. An hour later, Hitler's speech was on the placards and the crowds went home.

I was going now every evening straight from work in Australia House to sit for about one and a half hours in the hall, waiting to get a seat in the House of Commons gallery. My cold, wet feet were soon warm in that place. One night the House was packed, every bench crowded, the atmosphere tense and dramatic. Mr Neville Chamberlain came in and with slow steps walked to his seat, where he sat with arms folded and head down the whole evening. I admired the thick iron-grey hair and the elasticity of his well-dressed figure. Winston Churchill sat a few feet away, sporting only a few poor wisps of hair upon his noble head. Lloyd

George sat opposite him, and his hair was long and straight and snowy-white.

The two pink bald heads of Sir Samuel Hoare and Sir John Simon clustered affectionately together close to the Prime Minister. I studied them all, the quiet dignity of Anthony Eden, the picturesque beauty of Sir Archibald Sinclair, Dr Summerskill's smartly curled auburn head, the sturdy figure of my favourite, Lieut.-Cmdr Fletcher, Stafford Cripps, Herbert Morrison, Mr Dalton, Greenwood and all. The debate was absorbing, noisy; I forgot everything else. I sat without moving though my bottom ached and my eyes burned.

Meanwhile the replies to my letters of application to editors began to arrive. Every single one was a refusal. But I was so excited to see the names of real-live editors, famous names, some of them, that I'd only read about, that I put the brief, sharp letters saying "sorry, no" away in a drawer as though they were treasures instead of the ending of my hopes. Well, it had been just a dream. And I locked the letters away and went back to dictation about buying and selling copper and brass for making tanks and guns and aluminium alloys for aeroplanes.

Miss Campbell, who was always called "the telephone", said, "Never mind, Oggi dear, I'm sure you will get into Fleet Street one day." Fraülein Pinkas, who was very intellectual and refused to listen to any music other than Bach, said she hoped so too because she felt I would never properly master German grammar.

With the Munich crisis over, business was picking up. Spring came early that year, and at lunchtime, when the daily screaming and shouting were over, during which the four men fixed a rock-bottom price to make a bid or an offer for tons of copper or brass, we strolled in the gardens of Savoy Place, now glowing with blue and purple crocuses.

Herr Friedmann was back in London to discuss some secret business which, it was whispered in the office, would keep us all for years to come. I devoured the evening papers and my cheese sandwich, and returned to the office to be told by an excited "telephone" that I was to be sent immediately to Warsaw to work there for Herr Friedmann.

I could not believe it. "But, Cammie, why me?" "Don't tell I told you," said Iris Campbell, "but I couldn't help hearing. You're to go in and see him now, so don't let on."

Breathless, I knocked at his door. For years now I had thought of nothing but how to be a reporter. Now this. And for me, humblest, most inefficient of all the shorthand-typists. "Ihr Deutsch ist furchtbar." The Herr Doktor used to go up close to little Berlinger and bellow it in his ear. "Her German is terrible! No more English ladies, please!"

Herr Friedmann was pacing his office in an agitated manner. He paused, looked up, then resumed his pacing, the while muttering in English and German. Was he perhaps making a big mistake in choosing this little girl for his biggest, most important assignment? "No, do not say anything. Just listen."

He needed someone with a British passport; someone whose badly-spoken German declared her of non-German origin. Ours was a secret mission, first to Poland, then to Greece and Yugoslavia, all those countries feeling themselves threatened by the Third Reich. I had to promise never to reveal to anyone, not even to my sisters, our destination. Also to promise never to speak any Russian while in Poland, as this was just as unpopular as German. Above all, to be "stumm" silent. Herr Friedmann put a finger to his lips. "There are many people in Sweden, Switzerland, France, who would like to make a counter offer to our customers . . . if only they knew the address."

I wondered how he knew it. I made my promises and ran back to join the girls. The office was suddenly silent. Yes, they were jealous. I felt it, and suffered. They had been so kind to me; they had gladly done all the work which was too difficult for me. For the timid "English lady" with the pale, thin, hangdog look and the shabby clothes.

Packing my small case and one dress and suit, I thought suddenly for the first time that I was glad I had not died in May 1937 and missed going to Poland in the summer of 1939.

CHAPTER XII

TO POLAND

WE HAD TO go the long way round by boat to Copenhagen and then a three-and-a-half hour flight, landing first at Gdynia. It seemed strange to be so close to Danzig, which had been in the headlines for the past months. I was still thinking in headlines, still trying to be the apprentice reporter.

We got back into the plane after the customs examination. Herr Friedmann said I must not forget to "schlucken" properly or I would get pain in the ear, as happened in the flight over the Baltic. Looking down, and remembering the £3 we had paid for excess baggage, I thought of Grandma and the children making the crossing for £2 and still having £1 left to enable them to land.

I was expecting something poor like the slums of Deritend and Aston. The heat came down on us like a blow in the face when we landed at Warsaw airport, and an unpleasant smell of cheap benzine. But the city was entirely beautiful, a city of flowers looking more as I imagined Marienbad or Salzburg to be than a big city.

Our hotel, the Europejski, and my balcony window faced a huge white square built in the Russian style when Poland belonged to the Czars. Each tall lamp-post carried an enormous tray of flowers round its middle, a sort of scarlet geranium that was not quite an English geranium, with a kind of white clematis. There were huge parks, immaculate with beds of quadruple scarlet gladioli and huge dahlias.

At noon each day I stood out on the balcony to watch the changing of the guard in the square, the soldiers in khaki and top boots. All the time there was the clatter of horses' hooves as the droshkys carried their fares round and round the white squares.

Because of the heat, riding in a droshky was more pleasant than a taxi. Herr Friedmann sat beside me in the little open cab, beaming at my astonished cries as we trotted up the Marshalkowska with its magnificent shops and stores. The Poles, I noticed, had even more chic than Paris. "Liebes Kind," he said, "you do not know very much."

I knew he was referring to the previous evening when we dined and danced under the sky at an open-air restaurant. The orchestra sat on a circular stage in the middle of lawns filled with small tables. It was the best time because of the appalling heat. In our party were a number of beautiful blonde girls and young men who were officials of the Polish Government factories like the Panstwowe Witwornie Uzbrojenie "Tissa". Several, who spoke some English, told me they were Roman Catholic. I was shy about accepting their invitations to dance because of my old black dress. Their girls were elegant in silk dresses, low-cut and sleeveless, and they wore big, expensive straw hats on silky hair wound round their heads. Herr Friedmann said I must of course dance. "It is good for their English."

Driving back in the droshky to the hotel, the strains of "La vie en Rose" followed us. I told him I had never before seen people as beautiful as these Poles.

"They are German refugees," said Mr Friedmann. "Most of those you met tonight are Jews or half-Jews. I knew their parents in Berlin and Köln."

"No, they are Catholics," I told him.

"Liebes Kind," said Herr Friedmann absently.

In the days that followed we visited many of his friends and "customers" by droshky. Every hotel window, every shopwindow, every house and flat even in the meaner streets, and from ground-floor to the topmost storey had its own window-box of bright flowers, and the window-boxes were so large that one could hardly see any window but only masses of flowers.

We lunched on iced borscht with thin-sliced cucumber and strings of the greenest parsley, on chicken with sweet carrots, sweet beer and compote, and drank fine Herbata (tea).

One evening I was told to be ready for a grand Rundfahrt in a friend's car. This was to be for my benefit but, meanwhile in the back of the car, Herr Friedmann and the friend would discuss business. It was a huge Daimler-type car and, sitting in front with the driver, I could not hear the conversation, except that it was in German and almost in a whisper. The friend was a huge, tall cripple, an old, old man who had to be carried from the car and who could not walk unaided. I could just distinguish, under a large homburg hat, a white, tormented face. Herr Friedmann spoke about me jokingly to the stranger, who was addressed as "Herr Professor". It was pointed out that I was very English, and that I thought all Poles were the most handsome people in the world. "Typisch englisch," I heard Herr Friedmann chuckle. "Shocking German, worse French, even in English she makes mistakes, but she is a nice girl and she likes Poland."

The huge black bulk at the back of the car shifted uneasily. "Why is she called Olya, Olyechka?" he asked, using the Russian diminutive of my name. Herr Friedmann laughed and said it was because the English were known to be great eccentrics. They liked outlandish names, for example. But English girls had nice manners, he said, and did not answer back.

That disposed of me. We rode softly along miles of great, wide, tree-lined avenues on either side of the River Vistula. We heard the soldiers singing as they crossed the bridge in mass formation and marched off into the darkness. Then we drove through the enormous Jewish quarter, slowly through the hot, crowded streets. I saw there were only Jews on the streets, and these so crowded that the car could scarcely pass; on between brightly lit, wide streets and mile upon mile of busy shops; bearded Jews with round black hats and black cloaks were there, young and old.

August began with an even more intense heat. The blazing sun seemed to hurt the air. Yet outside, throughout the morning of 6 August in the great square facing us, there were parades in full-dress uniform, and officers in blue cloaks and high, blue hats marched to commemorate the twentieth anniversary of Poland's independence under Marshal Pilsudski. As though there were not enough light and heat already, the soldiers lit two great stone torches and the people sang and the loud-speakers howled while we tried to work through this on long, long specifications for armaments.

Warsaw was intensely gay that summer, despite the African heat. Every night our Polish and other friends called at the hotel to take us out to dinner and dance. Now and then Herr Fried-mann had business discussions with Polish Government officials, and he would vanish to some secret destination for the whole evening. I was left in charge of a blond young Pole named Tadeusz Wdowinski. On Sunday afternoons, he took me to the large, gay bathing-pool and after swimming we all lay sun-bathing and listening to the music from the loud-speaker; "Music Maestro, please".

At nine o'clock in the evening we joined the same large party as always at the Café Royal, drank wine and vodka under the trees, and danced under the open sky until midnight. Sometimes Herr Friedmann wanted to have meat, and as it had to be kosher for him we went to the open-air Jewish restaurant and had noodle soup and kalbsbraten with gurken and peas and compote of many fruits.

Sometimes Tadeusz Wdowinski called for me on his motor-cycle and we rode out into the flat fields of the countryside where the gypsies lived. Several times the Herr Professor, the strange cripple, called for us in his car. He was an extraordinary figure in huge cloak and hat in the terrible heat of the night.

I hoped it would all go on forever. After the lonely room in St John's Wood it was like a dream. And I knew that it would be hard to go back there, after this.

The next Saturday the crippled stranger took us in his car to Constantin. A great white house stood among woods, in the kind of green "glush" that Pushkin has described when Onegin meets Tatiana at her home in the remote countryside. A young man sat at the piano, surrounded by a rapt, silent audience and played Chopin hour after hour. White-capped and shawled servants ran to carry the cripple into the house and prepared to serve us dinner. I slipped out into the woods while it was still light. Sniffing the earth and grass and trees, I understood why Grandma had deserted England to flee back to her home village.

Herr Friedmann was both elated and disturbed on returning to the hotel in the early hours of the morning. The "business" was now almost concluded. If we worked, he with the calculations and I with the typing, all the next day, we could have the first contracts ready for the Government signatures. We had sold them vast quantities of copper and brass semi-manufactured materials for making heavy tanks and guns. The goods were to be supplied by the British firms of Imperial Chemical Industries and Enfield Motors and by the American firm of Bethlehem Steel. The orders ran into millions of dollars, and at least one-third had to be paid for in advance by first-class letter-of-credit to be deposited at a New York bank.

Then why was he so nervous? Because he had heard ("No, do not ask me how for I cannot tell you") that there might be war this weekend. And since that Monday and Tuesday were a Bank holiday in Poland, many business houses would be closed—some for the whole week.

There was no steamer for Copenhagen for several days, and all planes there were fully booked up, with not one seat to be had. Supposing war should come suddenly, he would be trapped. There was only one other way out of Poland, and that was across Germany, where he would be arrested immediately.

Next day was yet another holiday festival. All morning the soldiers were once again putting up the flags in the square. Then the marching began, as it always did early in the morning, and the brass bands joined in. At the military headquarters facing the hotel, the guard was changing in its setting of white flowers. Throughout the night the regiments marched and sang, swinging lighted torches in the hot darkness.

For the next few days I sat typing the whole day and night. Each night it was after midnight when Herr Friedmann returned. The contracts were signed. There were only a couple of days left to the end of August. He was in a state of great agitation.

He had been told that the war would begin in the next few days. Even tomorrow might be too late. Tadeusz Wdowinski had gone to try and get us two seats on tomorrow's plane to Denmark. We should have to work through the night.

It was nearly dawn when the phone call came from Tadeusz. He had two seats for us. We must leave immediately.

At 8.30 in the morning we stood in a daze in the morning heat. Herr Friedmann was telling Ted, as I called him, that somehow he would get an affidavit signed to enable him to flee to England. He would do it the first hour he arrived in London. A young man named Kraftlos stood with us, his eyes never leaving Herr Friedmann's face. He was a former employee from Süss & Friedmann's old Berlin office who had escaped from Germany and was found starving in Krakow. Herr Friedmann sent for him on our arrival in Warsaw. He put him in a room in our expensive hotel, plied him with money, food and clothes, found him a job and someone to look after him. He was one solid mass of worship for Paul Friedmann. I could see that any moment poor Kraftlos was going to weep.

As our plane rose slowly in the simmering air, we stood at the windows waving to our friends below. Their faces were upturned to us and they were waving, not smiling.

Not many more days after that, our Hotel Europejski was a heap of rubble. The flowers were gone too; and the water-carts which used to roam the streets through the night, to pour water through big hoses on to the city of window-box flowers, were seen no more.

CHAPTER XIII

WAR

IT WAS A quiet war at first. My landlady and her friend were upset when they had to register for gas-masks, because they were asked to give their ages.

One of the Fraüleins always carried her gas-mask with her to the lavatory. Herr Friedmann insisted that we should take our gas-masks out to lunch with us, but we kept forgetting or leaving them in cafés in the Strand.

My landlady, Mrs Mann, shook like a leaf every time the air-raid siren wailed. It was very loud in St John's Wood, and some warnings sounded at three o'clock in the morning. Mrs Mann worried, too, about her only son Cyril, who stalked the streets outside, with gas-mask and tin helmet jammed flat on his head.

In those first weeks it was stifling while the hot weather lasted. Every time the warning began, Cyril stormed into my little £1-a-week bed-sitter and closed my window; Mrs Mann moaned "Cyril, Cyril" over and over. It was no use trying to leave by the front door because the Wardens simply ordered you back indoors.

By 6.30 each evening restaurants closed. So did milk bars and tea-shops, while staff at all public buildings locked their doors and blacked out their windows. At Metal Supplies Ltd, however, we were still working each night until we were ordered out and the lights were turned off. There was nothing else to do but board a bus and go home in the darkness, pointing one's torch carefully in order not to waste the battery.

So the war began, and we settled down to it. A kind of hush fell over the firm of Metal Supplies. Franz Josef Süss moved his children and his Catholic wife out to Surrey; the Friedmanns stayed where they were. The Australian Government said they wanted our offices on the third floor, and as the lease was up there was nothing else to do but to look for a new place. We moved into a building in Chancery Lane, but things were never the same after that. No more hour-long calls to the Continent, no more tears from Herr Berlinger because he had been "cut up"; no more shouting from the Herr Doktor, who sat eating salt-beef sandwiches and poring over old files and old contracts. Miss Campbell had joined the WAAF, and we missed her telling us about her love affair and how she was going to tell Herr Süss what he could do with his job if he dared to comment at her being more than half an hour late in the mornings.

I was too depressed even to write any more applications for jobs on newspapers, or magazines. What was the use? I took out of the locked drawer all the replies and refusals—a large pile—which I had to date. I wanted to see if there were a note of hope in any one of them so that I could try again. True, some had said "we will keep your name in front of us", etc. But the editor of the *Daily Herald* had written that in order to work on a newspaper I had to belong to the National Union of Journalists. And in order to become a member of that Union, I had to work on a newspaper. Deadlock.

I knew the mood would pass and that I should try again. Meanwhile there was Herr Berlinger to cheer us. We met on the stairs one day and walked up the Strand together. Yes, it was depressing, he agreed. No business. He'd like to get married too, but where did you find the right girl?

And out it all came, his story. We had all wondered. We were very fond of him, for he was kind and comic too, with his big-eyed clown's face, the large head protected by thick bristle which he was always scratching.

She must be very beautiful, he said, and very, very fromm

(religious) and very rich indeed. Of course, he had had his chances. One beautiful girl had followed him all the way from Paris to Amsterdam, and another, even more beautiful, had chased him from Switzerland to London, and there had been another one in Le Touquet beautiful as a dream who was offered with francs worth £7,000, but when he had worked it out with the French franc at the present rate of exchange it only came to £5,000 and he had to turn it down. "All the women are out to catch me," said the little man, "but I am too smart to be caught."

I said if he would wait a moment I would put on some lipstick and see what he thought about the result. "And I can cook." I said.

Herr Berlinger looked at me fearfully; his expression was startled. Then he recovered. "Ha ha! You English ladies you make always good jokes, yes! Ha ha!"

Ha ha yourself, I said but when I got back to the office I made the girls sick with laughter so that we could not work, any of us. So we cheered up a bit.

The only business for us was our continuing work on the long, long contracts concluded with the Polish Government for which we had been paid. Only now there was no Polish Government or even any Poland.

Herr Berlinger came in then. Would I like to go out with him on Sunday? I said I was sorry I had another engagement. "Never mind," he said kindly, "you are very beautiful. It is great pity that you are not good Jewess and not rich."

One day Fraülein Behrend and I received a visit from our old colleague Miss Campbell, our beautiful blonde telephonist. She was now Aircraftwoman (1st Class) Campbell of the WAAFs, and she was unhappy.

Over an evening meal in the Strand Corner House, Iris Campbell told us her story. The trouble was that Iris, like all of us with Metal Supplies, had had a comfortable time. Her job at £3 10s a

week had been specially easy because she was the only "real
English lady" among us. Iris used to stroll into the office at 10 a.m.
If ever a gentle word of protest was made to her, she stormed.
How dared these foreigners reprimand her? Not that she had ever
been reprimanded. About once in four months Herr Süss, scarlet
with blushes and trembling all over, would implore her to make
a special effort for his sake. After that he would make a great fuss
of her all day in case he had been too harsh. And now? Life in the
airforce was a nightmare for poor Iris.

Her day now started at 7.45, and drill in the cold damp Essex
air lasted until 9 o'clock. The first offence of being late was over-
looked, the second offence, which occurred only that week, was
punished with fatigue duty. Campbell, as she was then called,
being just a ranker, had been only two minutes late, she told us.
"In fact, I was already in the room and in time for when my name
was called, but I'd been spotted coming into the room when roll-
call had already begun. I was spotted and reported. My fatigue
duty consists of spending this weekend, which would normally be
my free-time, scrubbing floors and cleaning out flues."

Fraülein Behrend and I were shaken. Our Iris, who had never
done anything tougher than launder her ninon nighties. "A third
offence means four weekends scrubbing."

"They keep saying to us 'You're in the army now, you know'.
We work three nights a week until seven, usually until eight
or nine on the whim of the assistant-commander. Over-
time is not paid for. We get 2/2 per day, and the food is so
poor that all this goes on filling-up. The cold is terrible, and some
of the girls have to work in icy hangars, quite unheated. Our
promised uniforms have not arrived . . . after three months!
So we only have shirt-blouses and skirts to wear and a blue coat
which is the weight and warmth of a mackintosh with no proper
lining to it."

Iris asked permission to wear her own navy sporty coat, which was at least warm and heavy. Her request was turned down. Her lovely blonde curls, of which she had been so proud, had to be worn pinned severely into a bun.

We listened, horrified. Yes, we said, we would plead with Herr Friedmann to take her back if she could plead ill health and resign. Iris, who had always been a spirited girl and our leader in Metal Supplies, had tears in her eyes. We could see that the thought of our office, with the little electric fire we had wangled out of the electrician, our gossips and our tea and biscuits, and all our little privileges and comforts, even the noisy foreigners she had despised, seemed to her now an unattainable paradise. Not to mention the £3 10s a week.

The Herr Doktor sent for me about several mistakes in grammar. "Zis cannot be," he said, but there was no fire left in him. We knew well enough that Süss and Friedmann were keeping us all on simply because they knew and we knew there was nowhere for us to go. After all, it was a pretty static war so far. "All right," said the Herr Doktor, closing his files for the day, "go with God."

Fraülein Behrend said, "We really ought to do something about Dr Mayer's terrible English. He keeps saying 'zis and zat' instead of 'dis and dat'."

I stared through the window of our Chancery Lane office at the pouring rain. The Thames was running higher. I was only a few yards away from Fleet Street now. Yet I seemed further away than ever. How much longer must I wait and hope and try in vain?

I was nearly 28. Soon it would be too late. Too late to train in the writing business. Too late to write the book Father had wanted to write, or have me write for him.

CHAPTER XIV

FLEET STREET AT LAST

ONE DAY I got home from the office to find a letter. It was from the most important news agency in Fleet Street, from the great firm of Reuter. And it said, "Referring to the application which you sent us eighteen months ago, please would you call for an interview . . ."

At last. Oh, it was a very humble start. The charming editor said, no, he didn't mind that I'd had no experience in journalism. No, he didn't mind anything. All the men were being called up, you see. They would have to wait and see what I could do. And for a start, could I make a big, hot pot of tea?

In fact, those first weeks and months proved to me that all my dreams and ideas about journalism had been a lot of nonsense. Being a journalist didn't mean having a fine prose style and good spelling. It meant that, when the chief sub-editor was piecing together a splash story for the morning papers—using Agency cables and eyewitness accounts telephoned from abroad about the bombing of Rotterdam, say—what he most needed was a girl who could run upstairs to the library, to get all the basic details about Rotterdam from books and maps and gazetteers and files, and race downstairs with it quick as quick; someone who could read his shorthand and type it all out, putting in the bits he might have forgotten, and race to the teleprinters with it. Journalism then was just this: being in the right place at the right time, with the right information.

It wasn't much, but it was a start. I did not realise then, on those endless sixteen-hour night duties, that this was something of a

E

false start too. Journalism, I was to learn much later, could never
be done sitting down.

Meanwhile there were the heavy jugs of tea to be made and
carried round. At least I was in the right place, even if not yet
doing the right job. Only after the night's bombing was ended,
about six o'clock in the morning, when a grey light came behind
the blackout curtains, when the morning editions appeared on our
table and the sub-editors were checking what the papers had done
with their stories . . . then my proper training would begin in the
two or three hours remaining before we went off duty. We were
doing a double shift to avoid going home during the bombing
raids. That was why we needed so much tea, to keep us awake.

Michael Fry, a clever and frightening young man, was given
the job of trying to teach me. Now and then he went into a kind
of trance, partly from boredom and partly because he believed
that certain Yoga exercises would rejuvenate him. He would suddenly stand on his head, or lie flat on the long green desk as though
he were dead.

"All right, let's see what you've done with the Burma com-
muniqué. No, that's no bloody good."

He said it was useless to try and be a journalist unless you had a
nose for news. "It's all in the nose," he said pointing at his own
long one, then, taking a savage pull at mine, "Every story has got
to have a nose."

Write your headline first, he taught me. So the 14th Army
advanced two miles, then that's your headline and that's your
story. All the rest is padding. You put it in afterwards lower down.

At midnight we had an hour off, to lie on a divan and sleep
in the dark basement. But it was stifling there. So I went up to the
fourth floor to talk to the Russians in Tass, the Soviet news
agency. Here I felt strangely at home.

There was Rogov, a fat square man who was the editor-in-
charge. He had been the Tass man in Peking for a number of

years, and later became editor of *Izvestia* for a short time. Rogov
was interested chiefly in sex. He said that Chinese women and
Englishwomen were the best for his purposes, and they should
preferably be over forty-five years of age. Once he showed me a
photograph of one of his favourites. "But she is old," I said with
all the tact and perceptiveness of a woman under thirty. Besides,
you could say anything to Rogov and if you did not say out-
rageous things he quickly became bored. "Of course she is old,"
he said. "She is also very grateful."

Most of the work he left to his underling, a shy little man named
Mikhail Basharin. I used to talk to Misha about Grandma and all
our potty Russian relations. He was fair and good-looking in a
tired, faded sort of way, and always had a warm smile revealing a
mouthful of dark grey steel teeth.

Basharin and I were close because he wasn't a real journalist
either, though he pretended to be, and he always sat about
clutching the long sheets of news-tape as though they were a sort
of lifeline, even taking them with him to the lavatory. He'd been
a schoolteacher in Moscow and then a factory worker, and had
earned the journalism job in London as a reward for good work.
He had four small children, a tired wife, a tiny flat in Notting
Hill and very poor health. He showed me his snaps of the family
and I showed him old photos of the Izvozchik couple, Grandma
and Grandpa.

I told him everything. What a failure Grandpa had been as a
travelling glazier; how Grandma, homesick for her village, had
insisted on their going home to Russia. How they'd found the
door of their old home bolted and the dogs barking in the yard.
And how a silly uncle who lived there with a new wicked wife
shouted through all the fourteen windows, one after the other,
that they could all go back to England and starve, for all he cared.
And back they'd all come a second time, with not a rag nor rouble
between them then. And Aunt Becky had started to be born

right there on the docks at Grimsby, among all the poor immigrants lugging their bundles and the fishermen hauling the great nets of cod ashore and the steam train hissing in the station.

Little Basharin, upstairs in the canteen at No. 85, Fleet Street, smiled at all this, showing his steel teeth over the cracked cup of awful tea. We usually ate together, mostly sandwiches of the evil-smelling cheese; evil because it was already terribly old. But Basharin and I hardly noticed the terrible cheese and the sugar-rationed tea. Because now we were both journalists and this was what we both wanted. He made me tell my story again and then he sighed and even cried a little once, because he was so sorry for me.

But why, Misha, I said, why should you be sorry for me, Misha? I was astonished, for I had stopped being sorry for myself, oh, a long, long time ago.

And he said it was because he believed I was a real, true Russian at heart, and I belonged to Russia and I had lost Russia forever.

"Bednaya," he said, "bednaya, Olyechka, you poor thing."

CHAPTER XV

AUNT BECKY AGAIN

It was Lily B. who found me new digs, a tiny room and full board for 37/6 a week in Canfield Gardens, between West Hampstead and Swiss Cottage.

This was a well-run boarding house operated by a mother and daughter. The Morleys had returned from years abroad in Buenos Aires, only to be caught up in the war with not enough money to live on.

I met Lily through Aunt Phoebe and Aunt Sally. For the bombs now falling upon London were the means of bringing some of our long-lost relations together for the first time in many years. We gathered especially on Friday evenings at my cousin's flat in Grove End Gardens. There was Aunt Sally, who came when she was not at a séance. There was Cousin Rozlie, Phoebe's eldest, who was famous in our family for being like Aunt Becky. That is, she was very clever and a good linguist. She was also unmarried. Aunt Becky herself was also on her way to us, now a refugee from Pilsen, Czechoslovakia, with her husband Uncle Ernest Adler and their little daughter Betty.

It was indeed an ingathering of the Izvozchik clan, this time the female end of it.

All the "girls" in our group were unmarried also. They included Phoebe's younger daughter Rita Cave, who had small parts in BBC radio plays. Then there was Lily, Cousin Roz's friend, and there was Uncle Abe's daughter Jane, and her friends Mitzi and Phyllis and Sylvia and Anne.

And now, incredibly, among us was Aunt Becky, who still bore traces, I thought of a condemned spinsterhood in spite of having a husband and daughter. Could this be the intellectual virago who had haunted our childhood? This mild, blonde, pedantic little woman?

I told her rather daringly, Father's story of her birth at Grimsby after being thrown out by the wicked uncle at Utyena. Even the baby had been fed cod liver oil, for they had nothing else.

"It was all the cod's fault," I said, a bit nervous, meaning to make a joke of it and missing, but still hoping she would be flattered. Father had blamed the cod and its oil that made Becky grow up so clever.

This brought quite a lecture from Aunt Becky. It dealt with the foolishness of primitive peasants from Russia who could not read or write. It disposed of the discredited theory that there was some link between the brain and the phosphorus in fresh fish. "Your Father talked too much", said Aunt Becky. "The cod didn't do anything for his brain, evidently. I was highly qualified because I went to a university and I was the first of our family to do so."

Aunt Becky spoke Czech as well as French and German. Aunts Phoebe and Sally kept quiet. There was the same lack of communication between the sisters as, years ago, I had seen between the brothers. They had the same habit as Abe, Mo and Izzy of not addressing each other directly but always through a third party.

"I don't know what your Aunt Becky plans to do now," said Aunt Phoebe, addressing me.

"We certainly don't want to be a burden on anyone," said Aunt Becky, also addressing me, as though the sisters were speaking a foreign language and I was the interpreter who had to pass the message on.

Meanwhile Phoebe's elder daughter Rozlie was discussing the situation of Aunt Becky and her family, in the same indirect way, with Aunt Sally.

"We should let Uncle Mo know in Birmingham," said Rozlie.

"Mo," said Sally, "is at Bournemouth for his kidneys."

It was like being at home, a girl again, in that un-cosy nest of uncles sitting side by side at the tea-table, each pretending the other was not there.

Still, it was a haven of warmth for me, compared with the boarding-house where retired ladies complained about the rations. Most evenings were devoted to the only topic that mattered, and it had nothing to do with the war or refugees. All the girls were in their late thirties or early forties, so there was no time to lose.

Lily was my favourite. She was crude, outspoken, but warm and unselfish. Aunt Sally, frankly shocked, went home when Lily started talking about the men in her life.

Aunt Sally and I had a special status as guest-members in this lonely-hearts club, because, as respectable widows, we too were felt to be deprived. Also we were the only ones who could cook or clean out dirty pans.

None of my cousins Roz and Rita and Jane Davis—not even Lily—could do any domestic work or cooking. Jane could cook but wouldn't. Rich Uncle Abe had not been on speaking terms with her because of this. He thought if she wouldn't cook or do something then she ought to get a job, but Jane thought it was rather disgraceful for a wealthy man's only daughter to go out to work. Jane Davis felt that if she took a job it might encourage her Father to believe that meanness paid, so she didn't get one.

Roz and Rita had always been waited on. Rita said, "It's Grandma's fault, for being such a snob."

Rita was keen on what is now known as "show-biz", and very ambitious. Then came a set-back. She was dropped from a BBC radio show because, it was claimed, she couldn't yodel. But Rita had not only our Grandmother's snobbery but also her determination. She persuaded all her friends to write letters of protest to the BBC complaining "What has happened to Rita Cave?" The letters poured in at such a rate that in the end our Rita was hauled before the Board and had to admit she had largely prompted this voluminous correspondence. Undaunted, Rita formed her own talent-spotting agency and worked at it in a frenzy. She was full of pluck. On the very day she died, she was phoning all the papers about a new find, a Miss Nyree Dawn Porter.

On the next Friday, when the lonely-hearts group all met, we discussed what Lily should do about Dick, who showed no signs of marriage.

"I've told him," Lily said. "I made an ultimatum. Seven years, I told him. 'I've given you seven years of my life.' Now is the time for him to declare himself."

Lily had a lovely voice, and could use it to full dramatic effect.

"What did the swine say?" asked Rozlie.

"He will let me know in a fortnight."

Rozlie was going to comment, then thought better of it. Not, her face, always an expressive one, seemed to say, not in front of our provincial cousin.

But Lily rushed on. Lily knew about my unsuccessful, brief affair with a dispensing chemist. This put me on the right footing in the group, Lily felt.

"Now you're really one of us," Lily told me kindly, "now you've been ditched. Men are such bastards."

The Girls had a large number of sundry hangers-on, admirers, casual and serious suitors, refugees. These were known to all of us as "bloody deutschers". This was partly because as suitors they didn't rate, being concerned apparently with the act of survival rather than the act of love leading to a possible marriage. Also their German origin was unpopular, which showed how illogical and unfair were women who were more concerned with getting a husband than human justice. I had a certain slight cachet in the group of Girls whom I named the Lonely-Hearts, because my in-laws were French citizens who had not yet had to flee from Paris. So I decided not to mention that the older ones had been born in Poland and had carp floating in the bath.

I became popular as tea-maker and companion. I was made specially welcome on the odd nights when no one came. Sometimes, unaccountably, the admirers vanished. The reluctant suitors, who included the divorced, the widowed, a number of elderly bachelors, even one homosexual, and also, according to Lily, one of un-identifiable sex and one avowed impotent, just failed to turn up. Perhaps it was their bath nights, Lily said. But the Girls did not like empty evenings without company, and when the bombs began to fall upon London they liked to have a full house because an empty one could, they felt, affect their status as Popular and Sought-after "Girls".

There was the new girl, Kitty. Kitty was young and virgin and nice. She was Rozlie's new lodger in a room much sought after, as it was on the ground floor and safe from bombs and blast. Lily was interested in Kitty, who, after courting a boy for eight long years, had just received an invitation from him to his wedding with a very rich Girl.

"Scab," said Lily, handing back the invitation card after careful examination. Lily said that we all ought to join the Marriage Bureau in Bond Street. "You pay £5 down before you can register, and £20 down on getting a husband. Or else the man pays, if he can afford it. You specify what kind of man you want to meet, and an appointment is arranged."

It was decided that Lily should go the next night and Rozlie after that. And Kitty must be forced to go. "And you too," said Lily to me, "you stand quite a good chance. Some men prefer a nice juicy widow."

Rozlie said that if I didn't have the fiver they'd make me jolly well save up until I did. She went to telephone Rita to put a fiver aside in this good cause. While I went to make the tea Lily telephoned her mother. "I know it's a lot," said Lily in her lilting voice. "But it's all in a good cause. I'd think you'd even pay a lot more, Mother dear."

Having settled that, we all got down to the business of the details. Should each one specify on the application form Jew or Gentile? The Gentiles were preferred, for one thing they were so far untried, untested to any great extent. After that we dealt with the desired height, weight, income and habits we required. Rozlie said she'd put down a widower of forty; Lily wanted a large, fat man with pocket-book to match. "I couldn't look at a thin man," said Lily shuddering. Kitty, giggling, also specified widower, possibly with children, and she was willing to waive the "love" clause, if there were one, in the marriage specification.

Sylvia, a glamorous neighbour along the corridor, was a qualified hairdresser and had bought her own hair-dryer. This became a popular way of spending the evenings when the bombs were being unloaded on the West End of London. Anyone who was nervous was given a hair-do and popped under the hair-dryer and left until the all-clear. You couldn't hear a thing under it. Even when our building got hit and two upper floors of the block just caved right in, the girl under the dryer knew nothing until we took her out of it.

Rita was the business woman among us. She was then a personal assistant to Oscar Deutsch, who owned the Odeon organisation. It made her very haughty. "Call yourself a journalist," said Rita to me, "and you don't know anybody." She was dining at the Dorchester with the Kellinos. That made me think. Rita was right. I was, it often seemed to me, a non-starter in journalism. Working in the Agency on war communiqués, it was rare to be sent out to interview anyone. I had only been sent on one assignment, so far. That was to interview Oswald Mosley. But when I handed in the story it got reduced to three lines, which seemed to me worse than not being sent on the story at all.

"I've got to have a new coat and costume and you've got to give me the coupons, Rosie," Rita said. The atmosphere became very tense when Rozlie said **no**, she needed them for her little millinery business. She hated being called Rosie. It was a reminder somehow of poor little Rozie Izvozchik, who had sung for the family supper in the streets of Grimsby, and sewn shirts "in poverty, hunger and dirt".

Aunt Phoebe sat in a low chair. In her seventies now, she was a pathetic figure, and so deaf that the Girls were able to discuss her without her taking in a word. She rolled unsteadily when she crossed the room, "Nichevo matushka," said Rita trying to steady the poor woman. Rita was the only one who was not actually ashamed of our Russian origin.

Rozlie said that was because Rita was in "show-biz", which had lots of peculiar people in it.

I felt I was a cheat now. There I was, making tea for the Girls, listening to them and making sympathetic clucking noises when they talked of the husbands they one day hoped to achieve. It was cheating because now I no longer shared their hopes and fears. Something had happened to me, almost without my knowing it. I felt like a free woman visiting a harem, happy to escape into the outside world. Marriage, home-life no longer interested me. I wanted to live by my own labour as a human being instead of as a woman. And surely the place to find this free working life could only be in Fleet Street? I still believed it, then. As the war flamed around our walls at No. 85, Fleet Street, in those years.

Our landlady in Canfield Gardens, West Hampstead, Mrs Morley, a handsome, white-haired, straight-backed woman, was a disciplinarian. It was hard work for her and her daughter to feed us all fresh hot meals in spite of rationing and air-raids. So she had no time for some of the older, retired ladies who sat knitting or reading and waiting for the next meal.

I was embarrassed as one of the "workers" to be given second helpings when others were refused. Mrs Goodman suddenly burst into tears late one night when I was on my way to bed.

"I've never been so unhappy in my life. They all hurt me, they say things to hurt me and I can't be hurt. I'm too tender. My husbands, you know, dear, I had two, they both adored me. I never asked for such idolatry . . . and now, such hardness, such coarseness, oh oh!"

I patted her plump shoulder and said "Never mind", but she sobbed so hard that I was afraid Mrs Morley, who slept downstairs, would hear it. The door opened, and Mrs Morley came in wearing a dressing-gown.

"What's all the row? What's that you say? I'm unkind to you. Stuff and nonsense. It's all chaff. Now then, off to bed with you, and let's have no more nonsense."

The little woman stumbled towards the stairs. "I can hear my darling," she was muttering, "I can hear him saying to me, beloved, they're not fit to wipe your boots, such coarseness, you're too good, a tender angel like you, and all your lovely flesh melting away." Clearly, it had not passed everyone's notice that some people were getting second helpings and others weren't.

I could hear her still sobbing as I went to bed.

CHAPTER XVI

LILY AND THE LONELY-HEARTS

NEXT FRIDAY, AT the lonely-hearts club, I found a battle in progress. Lily, in figure-fitting pale blue, wore a determined air as she sat on the divan with Dick. He looked discomfited and toyed with a tea-cup.

Rozlie and Aunt Sally were still at the dinner-table, which was now placed in the hall, where it was safely away from any windows and therefore safe from flying glass, which was often a worse danger than bombs. They were craning their heads towards the half-open door, though. "When's it to be, Dick?" I heard Lily say in a firm voice.

"How can you ask me now," said Dick, "when I've got sinusitis? Sinusitis isn't a thing to be played about with, it's serious. *Now's* not the time to ask a man."

"It's always the wrong time to ask you anything," Lily said. "If you haven't got dermatitis and appendicitis you've got something else."

Dick sniffed and said nothing. Sally was humming in a casual way while busy listening and eating her salt fish at the same time.

"You offer me," said Lily with some drama, "the back-street of your life. Back streets, always back streets for me."

Lily and Dick had spent that afternoon at the cinema. It was on at the local Odeon, that new version of the Fanny Hurst novel *Back Street* with Charles Boyer and Margaret Sullavan in the main parts.

"Sinusitis or no sinusitis," Lily said, "if you don't make up your mind soon I'll leave you, Dick. I mean it."

"Will you?" said Dick hopefully.

"Seven years," Lily moaned, ignoring this interruption, "all of seven in a Back Street. God!"

Sally was giggling softly in the hall. Jacob served twice times seven for Rachel, these modern girls are so impatient.

Dick was retreating towards the door. He was a small pale-faced middle-aged man with a mop of black hair . As he appeared in the hall, where I sat with the others at the table, I gave him my practised version of a sweet, understanding smile. But Dick didn't seem to notice. He made for the door and was gone.

So the storm broke. Sally bent lower over her fish. I rushed to minister with the tea-cups. Lily was moaning that men are such swine. "He's ruined my life and now he walks out with sinusitis. Just like that." Her lipstick and mascara was all running together as the tears rolled. "The back streets," said Lily, weeping.

"Have some salt fish," said Rozlie.

I cleared away the meal and the remains of the stewed rhubarb and custard, and Sally put on her hat and coat to go home to her little flat opposite Lord's cricket ground.

Then we all sat down for a real session. Lily was telling us about a new boy-friend she had met recently. Such a surprising man. He had told her about his lame leg and his inferiority complex. Well, as it turned out he did have a lame leg, but the rest was patently false. For Lily, out of the kindness of her heart and be-lieving it to be her duty almost, had offered herself and been ac-cepted without much concern.

"Men are such swine," she said. "They kid you along they're almost virgins. Liars. Why he'd obviously had as much experience as I had!"

"But Dick?" I said.

No, Dick didn't know, of course. "Seven years, remember," said Lilly, "seven years in a back street." Lily lived with her mother in an elegant part of Hampstead.

Rozlie threw Lily a warning glance. It was a reminder that I was only a guest-member of the club and a bit simple at that.

"There's a bit of the salt fish left," said Rozlie.

I said, "I just had oxtail."

"Why can't we get married?" Lily was asking. "What's wrong with us, with all our gang? We've none of us done any good. Why? Where do we go wrong?"

"Marriage isn't everything," I said weakly. "I've got a cousin who knows a girl who's ever so unhappy."

"It's only the bloody Jews," said Lily. "Any freak of a girl can get a goy; they're too easy. Ah, how I hate Jews," she said.

"Yes," said Rozlie, "it's the men of our generation. They're rotten."

CHAPTER XVII

I AM FIRED

Now I FOUND that being in Fleet Street did not necessarily make me into a real journalist. On busy nights, when the fighting round Smolensk or at Alamein was most intense, I was given real work to do, though it was always much lesser in importance, like the war communiqués from Burma or China. "Here comes the Burma Queen," the boys would laugh when I came round again with the steaming mugs of tea. I told them I was sure I could find my way through the Burmese jungle without so much as getting my feet wet. It was tiring work with the Chinese army changing the names of all the rivers just as fast as I could cross them in the right atlas.

But when news was slack I was no more than a useful typist or runabout girl. I did not even have the status of a real journalist, and the Union refused to consider admitting anyone who was getting under the minimum rate of pay. It was the time of the big "dilutee" crisis. No one wanted to employ dilutee nurses or dilutee coal-miners or dilutee-journalists and yet there we were, diluting the work.

A word of praise from the night editor would cause me a quite unreasonable rapture. Then I was suddenly switched to the radio listening station at Barnet to take the German news in shorthand, which was in effect a kind of demotion. I was back at the beginning again. So I brooded, obsessed. I thought of Olive Schreiner's words. "Men and things are plastic; they move to the left and to the right when you come among them moving in a straight line to one end." Yes, but in which direction?

I was soon to find out. When my chance came, it was not at all what I expected.

For I became quite famous—in the only way it is possible to become really famous in Fleet Street—by being fired.

Our business, I had not realised, was quite different in this respect from other trades, like selling in a shop or travelling in frying-pans or insurance or something. In ordinary trades you need a reputation; you should be neat and clean, punctual, sober, hardworking, and not answer back. And if you've ever been sacked you don't usually mention it if you can help it.

But the news business, clearly, was quite different. In my provincial way I thought being fired was the end. Instead, for me, it was the beginning. One day Fleet Street had never heard of me, and the next everybody had. Very gratifying, I saw this later, but it did not occur to me at the time.

One of the rules of the Street was that you must not make little mistakes, but a really great big boob that gives everyone a laugh and something to talk about was all right.

The trouble came, just as in the old days when I was fired from a motor-cycle factory for bad German, from my imperfect knowledge of foreign languages. I was still no Auntie Becky in spite of Father's efforts. The only language I had ever really mastered was Russian, and French was always my special difficulty. Most of our news cables were in a terrible cable-ese French. Words were abbreviated and stuck together to save expense. The French was not at all the French they talk in France, or even in the lessons we had at King Edward VI High School in New Street, Birmingham. The cables came mostly from Buenos Aires, Rio de Janeiro and other capitals safe from the war.

So when a cable came through from Brazil saying that Mussolini's eldest son was going to box in a boxing match in Budapest, well it all looked all right to me. And all the other sub-editors were far too busy with the war news round Smolensk to bother about me and Mussolini's boy. It was the Russian front that mattered to the next day's newspapers now, and not the problems of the "Burma Queen".

Well, *The Times* editor liked that story of mine so much that he telephoned our news editor to send some more. And that's how it all came out that I'd got it all wrong and that Mussolini's son never raised a fist in any boxing ring in all his life. He was just going along for the ride. In no time at all our tapes were ticking it out madly all over town. Correction; correction!

Our chief, the late Walton Adamson Cole, sent for me and was really very nice. "Lovely story," he said. "Wish it had been true."

Then he said, "You know I've been thinking, you really might do better on the road."

And in a few weeks' time so I was, with his help and recommendation, of course—cycling round the lovely roads of Oxford and working as a reporter for the first time, on an evening paper, the *Oxford Mail*.

At long last, I was to get my training. At last it was going to begin.

CHAPTER XVIII

I BECOME A REPORTER

At least, it did seem like a real beginning, but that was only at first. I was humbly anxious to learn. Yet hardly a month passed before I realised that Oxford was not the place to learn the business.

For one thing, there was hardly any crime. The police court, I had been warned by well-trained journalists, was the schoolroom of good reporters. It was through a proper acquaintance with crime that one really learned to handle news. And there was almost none in the town and county of Oxfordshire at the end of 1943. Each morning I cycled eagerly from the boarding-house in Woodstock Road to the magistrate's court and took my seat on the little press bench and waited for something to happen. Every day it was the same thing. Offenders were accused of "committing a nuisance", which meant they'd had too much beer and were caught getting rid of it behind a wall. Or "riding a bicycle without a rear-lamp".

It was poor stuff for a girl who was keyed up to prove herself. The county court was no better; at night there were concerts in the colleges of Elizabethan madrigals or political debates for the undergraduates.

The town filled up quickly with American servicemen, and now the nuisances committed were of a different kind and were never mentioned in the police court. They attended lectures by Sir William Beveridge and queued up to thank "Sir Bill".

Our landlady cooked ham and cabbage for me and some Lancashire sergeants who were billeted on her. They had two phrases only, which they uttered at every meal. "Pretty," said the sergeants when their food was put in front of them. This, for some reason, always caused hoots of laughter from all. "D'you want to make sumink of it?" Everyone rocked with this sally, even the landlady.

Oxford in that October of '43 was mellow and golden and charming. It was lovely to cycle out to Headington for a conference of the Labour party. One speaker shouted out about Oswald Mosley and some fighting broke out, but it was soon over. Cycling home in the darkness, I kept a sharp lookout for rats, which ran across the highway at night, and were a great plague at that time.

It turned very cold, and it was icy in my little room when I rose at seven o'clock to hear the sergeants shouting "Eeeee's pretty" from the kitchen, so I knew that our monthly egg had arrived.

I was filled with impatience. What was I doing here trying to elude the Lancashire sergeants and the American ones, as well as the rats at night? I felt further than ever away from my goal.

Stymied again, I fell back on my old habit of writing letters and replying to advertisements in various papers. One day an offer arrived to join the reporting staff of the Newcastle *Evening Chronicle* on faraway Tyneside.

Newcastle was entirely different. Here was plenty of crime; even the Chief Constable himself was up on a charge in connection with some missing fire engines. There was enough violent assault, breaking and entering, rape, incest and carnal knowledge to keep any evening paper filled.

There was a dark raciness about this dockside town and its foreign seamen which emphasised the un-English and explosive atmosphere.

The day after my arrival a man occupying the next hotel room, who must have heard the tapping through the thin partition walked in while I was at breakfast and disappeared, taking my typewriter with him. The "hotel" was more of a boarding-house, and did not provide keys to the doors. Downstairs, in the basement, two sixteen-year-old kitchenmaids waged a constant war with an invasion of beetles. It was that kind of place.

The loss of my machine was a fearful blow. It was the only piece of "property" I possessed. It was all that I had left of Father, the one and only thing he left, except for debts, and had been bequeathed to me so that I could carry out my promise to write about the family.

But if Tyneside was full of crime, it was also full of efficient police. Within two days the thief was caught and my typewriter back in my wardrobe. It was a great relief. Now, if I couldn't learn the basic trade of crime writing here, then I never would.

Two people who were convinced that I was most unlikely to learn anything whatever were two newsmen of the old school, Percy Edwards, the chief sub-editor, and Arthur Wilson, the news editor.

"What can you expect?" said Mr Wilson in his bold Sheffield-accented stage-whisper, which seemed to me to carry as far as Wallsend dockyard. "These Londoners! No discipline. Fancy hats, that's all they know."

This was a reference to the confection of pale blue ribbon in which I had made my first misguided appearance and which, it was clear, was going to take some considerable living-down.

It was pointed out to Mr Wilson that I was a native of the city of Birmingham in Warwickshire.

"Well that's *South* too," said Mr Wilson. "Just riffraff."

"The thing is," said Mr Wilson, "what's her shorthand like? Can she read back her verbatim shorthand notes of the court proceedings?"

From that day forward I made it my business to see that I always could. Even though it meant forgoing a pleasant flirtation with police sergeants and detectives. But the afternoon encounters with Mr Percy Edwards were even more unnerving than Mr Wilson's strictures.

"Percy wants you", would strike terror in my heart on arriving back in the office from each day's court.

There he sat, a plump, still, almost oriental figure because of the unfathomable expression on the round owlish face, complicated by the thickly concealing spectacles.

"Have you your notes with you? Good. Will you kindly read aloud the alleged statement by defendant in the alleged false pretences case?."

In this way, slowly and painfully, I learned what journalism was when practised on this level; that is, the life of the daily court reporter in a provincial town. It meant that, if a man's name was spelt as Geoffrey when it should have been Jeffrey, there would be an angry visitor at our front door. Journalism was a series of traps into which you fell if you were not "experienced".

After only six months of this I was a veteran, sure-footed, confident. I made no more mistakes. From Percy I collected smiles. When he sent for me now, it was for a little chat. Mr Wilson too was affable and trusting.

Now I was fit . . . to be sent down a mine or out to Durham mining villages or chasing the young Prince Philip of Greece, who was working on a destroyer lying at Wallsend dockyard.

The boarding-house where I was a 52/6 paying guest was a house of Unhappy Marriage. "When I've made enough money out of you and my other boarders," said the landlady, "I shall leave him. He's jealous of my business because all the money goes into my own account. Never lifts a hand to help me."

Another unhappy woman boarded on the first floor. Mrs Womersley had been a dancer and a nurse, but she was afraid to take a full-time job in case "he just walks out". At weekends the husband went away with "other women" without a word, she said. After the evening meal Mrs Womersley wandered down to the kitchen to help with the washing-up and the conversation. "I hate men," she said, rubbing with a drying-rag at the plates and pans. "The only good men are dead ones, just like people say about the Germans."

She pushed back her dark hair, worn in a "freedom wave", as the local hairdresser, "Paule", called it. Wearing the blue dungarees she wore all day, she set out the cups for our evening tea. "I found in his pocket last night this . . . look . . . a bill for 18/11 for a pair of silk stockings, not for me."

She and the landlady became close friends. After tea and talk I climbed the stairs to my little room where, joyfully, I had for the first time in many years a little gas-fire and meter. The room was so small that I could sit on the bed and toast my toes at the popping blue and yellow flames.

On the way through the chilly corridor I passed the silk-stocking husband we had been discussing all evening. He was carrying a plate of sandwiches, for the pair fed themselves in their room. He was tall and dark and refined and in advertising.

The two rooms on either side were thinly partitioned from mine. I could hear the snores on the one hand and the nightmares on the other, suffered by a young seaman who had been torpedoed.

"Talk about your snorer," said the landlady, putting a plate of warmed ham and dried eggs before me, "I've got a Weeper in the next room. I went to see what was the matter. He's a young musician from Glasgow . . . that is, he's twenty-eight, if you please. Breaking his heart, would you believe it, because his father has just divorced his mother and married the other woman. Says his nerves have gone all to pieces. Can't even look at the piano any more. He's given up music to sell insurance policies. I could smell it, though . . . the drink. I told him he'd have to go."

The landlady's silent husband entered during these revelations. He listened carefully and went away in silence.

It amused me that the landlady had not spotted that I was "Jews". "I get all sorts, don't I?" she said. "I had an ENSA man recently, a Jew. He was so difficult with his food. Wouldn't touch pork or bacon. I couldn't be bothered with him, I can tell you. How am I supposed to know what Jews eat? I don't know any Jews."

I wondered what Father would have thought of two of my admirers. There was Geordie Howden, age 70, and Geordie Dobson, 69, silver-haired, and they walked supported by sticks. The landlady's unloved husband was very jealous. He knocked on my door. "There's two to see you," he hissed through the door. "Time you got yourself one young 'un instead."

So by day there was crime and misfortune in the magistrate's court, in matrimonial, juvenile, county, civil or Assizes. By night there was the constant struggle to get enough to eat and to keep warm in Utility clothing you could buy if you had the coupons. The winds on Tyneside did not merely blow; they lifted you, pushed you, whirled you indoors and out again through streets called Pudding Chares and Bigg Market, Pitti Mee, Tankerville Terrace, Quayside.

Our boarding-house had good fires, but you had to push your way roughly to the front. And, once safely there, you dared not leave, though my elderly Geordies fought to keep me a little place.

Mr Derek Porter said his wife would like to have me as a guest for 10 p.m. coffee. They were longstanding residents, and had the luxury of their own fire. I couldn't see the lady at first when I entered the room. It was no surprise to find her already in bed. The only way to keep even reasonably warm was to go straight to bed with a hot-water bottle, while keeping woolly socks and most of your clothing on.

On the bed sat or crouched or lay five enormous shaggy dogs. And seated on the pillow, as though conducting a doggy class, sat the sort of head boy, a very large hairy ape. Little Mr Porter, a very small man, was sitting between two of the dogs on one side of the bed. It wasn't until I saw Mrs Porter in a lacy nightgown sit up and lift the hairy ape towards her, with its arms clutching round her bare neck, that I realised. All the dogs and the outsize ape with its jointed shaggy arms were stuffed.

"Now do sit here and tell me about your interesting life." said the lady, patting a small empty space between the stuffed dogs. "You know, my dear, I can't live without animals and there is not a landlady in the whole of this wretched town that would allow me to have a dog in the house."

When I was sent to interview Prince Philip, he just groaned and said, "Oh dear, I never thought any of you people would catch up with me."

My Newcastle colleagues had taught me the right approach, usually "Howya, Ma" or "Howya, Hinny", which could be used for male or female interviewees. Only it didn't feel right in this case. Prince Philip of Greece, in the uniform of a Lieutenant in the R.N., was quite the handsomest man I'd ever seen. I was sweating slightly in my heavy long brown leather coat, the only relic of my former life in a leather business.

Mr Wilson had been given the "tip-off" that an important Prince was stationed somewhere in Wallsend dockyard. He called me in: "Get me that Greek Prince by tea-time and get on with it." I was overwhelmed once again with my usual self-pity. Why did I get all the tough ones? Like that time when a Soviet Russian sailor fell in the Tyne and was drowned while serving on a destroyer lying at Wallsend dockyard—one of those, that is, which were being loaned to Stalin under the lend-lease agreement. The ship's commander, Captain Ivanov, walked out in a terrible temper from the Coroner's court when it was stated that the Russian sailor had been drunk after an evening in the Turk's Head. I was the obvious choice to be "put on it", and for days I had to pursue the Captain, a stout little man with four children and a room with partial board in Gateshead, and never let him out of my sight until he'd given me, willingly or not, at least 800 words of why-he-didn't-agree-with the Coroner's verdict.

By this time I knew the reason why I got the tough ones. It was because I was a hard-news reporter now. Not a columnist or a feature-writer or a specialist, or better still a crime-reporter or an industrial one. An industrial man, for example, could have a comparatively comfortable time, because he could always say to Mr Wilson that he was terribly sorry he couldn't go out on any other story because he was already stuck with a Bevin-boy strike somewhere out in the County of Durham, or he had to sit in court all day for the case of the girl bus-conductors who refused to accept the war-time instruction to go and work in Birmingham. Our industrial man George Thompson said: "Specialise, girl, or your life won't be worth living."

Would a prince live in a hotel, say, or would he have his own palace? And, if he had his own palace, what on earth was he doing down at the docks? George didn't know either.

"Try all the hotels and boarding houses and the police," said Mr Wilson, booming from his desk at me. "Don't just sit there lass, get moving, don't hang about. Bless my soul, you young ladies, if I weren't here to put my foot after you . . ."

I could see right away, it was no use turning on the tears tap. Mr Wilson was the most tender-hearted man alive for a girl sick or in trouble. But if he suspected you were just trying to get out of a sticky job, he hounded you to the end. He kept coming into the news-room shouting, "Found the prince yet? Keep at it, girl, don't slacken the pace; keep pushing on."

It seemed unlikely that the Prince was staying at any of the hotels I knew, which were mostly around Jesmond Dene. Our hotel was full of Norwegian seamen, a few Finns and Greeks and, oddly enough, a Russian businessman from some unknown, un-named Soviet buying delegation who had taken me to the pictures one night to see "Demi-Paradise", which was all about a Soviet Russian innocent sent to England on a special mission. The story of the film (I think it was Laurence Olivier playing the Russian) affected him most strangely, and right there in the 3/9 seats I had the same struggle with him that I'd had with a policeman from the Newcastle City Constabulary, who told me one evening "I may be a policeman but I'm also a man you know".

At last I found the prince. He was staying at the Jesmond Hotel, which at six guineas a week, all found, was right out of our class; so I put on the leather coat and dashed off, thinking, and rather hoping too, that the whole thing was just a stunt.

The prince was out, they said at the desk. "No, sorry, hinny, we don't know a thing about him really. Just comes and goes. Yes, he is a real prince all right. It says so right here. No, we've no more princes, so he must be the one you're looking for, hinny girl. You'll just have to wait till he shows up."

When he came in, some hours later, there I was goggling at him and spluttering, "I'm from the *Chronicle*." I couldn't think of a thing to say. It was bad enough, I felt, having a prince down against your name on the day's news schedule, without his turning out to be a dream prince as well, with the sort of golden head and classic features always used to illustrate love stories in women's magazines. In fact, I couldn't even describe him coherently when I got back to the office, because he had been nice as well and I knew this meant that Mr Wilson would most likely send me back again to get some more chat. I wished I dared tell a lie and say the prince had thrown me out, instead of telling the truth, which was that, if we could obtain permission from the Admiralty and from his C.O., we could interview him if we really wanted to do so. "Well, hinny," said Mr Wilson, when I handed in my first descriptive piece about the prince, "I'd never have known you had it in you, its pure slush, girl, sentimental slush. Fairy-tale prince with violet eyes, my foot. That's what comes of going to all these slushy films. You just sit down and rewrite it and give me the facts. What did he *say*?"

The whole thing went on for weeks. I had to go back five times to see the prince. And he was nice and so polite each time, which made it worse. I could see he was sorry for me.

It made three neat little paragraphs on the front page, and I just hoped I shouldn't get any more princes because of all the nervous strain and not knowing what to say.

By this time I had to start thinking about how I was going to have myself launched once again in Fleet Street, now that I had done what the late Arthur Christiansen (*Daily Express* editor) had once told me was essential in our business, namely, to be properly trained on a provincial newspaper, for preference somewhere in the north. Well, now I was trained and ready . . . surely?

CHAPTER XIX

BACK TO FLEET STREET

IT WAS HARDER to get back to London than it had been to leave it. I wrote my usual—it was automatic now—letters begging an interview. I travelled up to Fleet Street and managed to get interviews with Gerald Barry and A. J. Cummings. The *Daily Mirror*, too, agreed to see an "Olga" who spoke Russian and whose name was the popular one then of Franklin. London was tense, receiving the so-called buzz bombs. But when I was offered an immediate job I hesitated. I told myself I ought not to let the Tyneside people down, that Mr Wilson trusted me, had patiently trained and suffered me. In reality, I think I was simply too timid still. Was I ready for Fleet Street yet? A timid girl in Fleet Street would be like a persistent virgin in a Turkish harem. It was the fatal flaw in me, which Father had always known about.

So I missed my chance. When I tried Gerald Barry again some months later, as it was the *News Chronicle* job I really wanted, they already had some other woman, a nice woman named Mabel Elliot.

The *Daily Sketch* agreed to give me a trial. This was then part of the failing Kemsley empire. For weeks and even months I sat around with nothing to do. No one in Kemsley House was interested in an Olga. Certainly not the foreign editor, a tall, rather sad-looking man named Ian Fleming; not our big chief Sidney Carroll, not his Lordship, but a chatty leader-writer noticed me. "I suppose you're one of these reds getting ready to seize power," he said. "They're all in the plot together. Who? Why, Winston Churchill and Stalin and Roosevelt and all the Jews." We had some interesting talks along these lines, but it didn't really compensate for having no work. I thought long-ingly of Newcastle and Gateshead, just across the river by the little tossing yellow tram, and I longed for the cosy police court and the full charge-sheet of Breaking and Entering with Intent, or Grievous Bodily Harm.

Then one day the news editor rushed in shouting, "Christ, Warsaw's been liberated and we haven't got a thing on it. Not a bloody line."

He was hitting his head with his hand like a clown in a circus. "I remember Warsaw," I muttered timidly in the silence that followed, as the reporters and the copy-taster and the feature-writers stood around watching Jack hitting his head over and over.

"What's that? Speak up . . . that girl over there."

My little piece went in the paper next day. It wasn't much, just an "I was there" piece of the kind quite out of fashion nowadays. But now the news editor knew where I sat . . . in the corner by a dirty map hanging by one drawing-pin from the stained and greasy wall. He knew my name and that my legs were all right. I remembered just in time to keep them well stretched out, showing my last pair of good pre-war silk stockings. Legs are something that every girl had got to have in the Street.

And within the next three days, before he could forget me, my big chance came.

"Hey *you*, Olga-from-the-Volga or whatever the russkies call you, there's someone downstairs with a possible story. See if there's anything in it."

Downstairs a little group of people were waiting for me as I stepped forward, armed with notebook and pen. They were not by any means my first refugees or repatriates in those early months of 1945. Even up there on Tyneside we'd had a variety of these. I'd been out on boats on freezing nights to meet them coming in . . . on Red Cross boats or on stretchers, unable to speak when you bent down and tried to get an interview.

But this was different. A tall, dark, good-looking young man came forward, holding a girl by the hand. He'd been a schoolboy of nearly ten years old, he told me, when his mother in Yorkshire let him go on holiday to stay with friends on the Continent. That was early in 1939. When the war came, he was trapped, a prisoner. He'd just got back, and now he wanted advice and help. He and the girl were to take the train from King's Cross that night, and there'd been no time to warn his mother. Would she believe he was her son? He was turned sixteen and looked twenty, a full-grown man.

"Look." He unfolded a photograph from his pocket. "That's me . . . when I went. All those years ago." I told him he'd just have to pretend until his mother got over the shock. To pretend he was still her little boy. Her Peter Pan.

Next day the paper splashed it, the snap of the little schoolboy, the full-length portrait of the tall young man and his girl. And, underneath, my story, Peter Pan goes home with Wendy.

The news editor was pleased.

I was in. At last.

"Bloody good story. Bloody quick work too," he said.

He was wrong about that, though. Six long years I'd waited for this. Not, in fact, so quick.

The problem, in those last eight months of the war, was to find a room or somewhere to live in London, still under bombs, broken and dirty and shabby.

England then was not a comfortable place to live, especially for a woman on her own who could afford only between £3 and £3 10s a week for rent. I was now accustomed to unheated houses and freezing bedrooms, and to having to compete with other boarders for the tepid bath on those days when the landlady permitted bathing.

But London lodgings were filled with the thing I feared most, the London mice. I moved from one dismal Notting Hill or West Hampstead room to another, all of which, priced at £3 10s a week, bore the scars not only of war and bombs and previous tenants but, for me more repellently, those of hordes of mice or worse. Sometimes I sat in late-night cafés or even in the office long after duty hours, simply in order to postpone the horrid moment of opening the door of my room, as noisily as possible to frighten the mice away, and meeting once again the musty odour of them, mingling with the damp and dust of fading, faded and badly damaged Victorian rooms.

Once I had a glorious month, occupying a £4-a-week room in a luxury flat belonging to an elderly Polish one-time opera star. There were no mice, it was clean, comfortable and centrally-heated. I had almost forgotten what it was like to be comfortably warm. But a series of night duties upset Madame and caused her favourite parrot to wake up at eleven o'clock each night when I returned from night-shift. The parrot awoke regularly, in spite of my almost silent stealth at entering the flat and shrieked out "Dammit!" over and over in that fearful raucous voice that healthy parrots have. The shrieks were followed by the even more intimidating sounds of Madame swearing at me in Polish, adding a fully-documented Polish version of my character which, even coming from the other end of the corridor, sounded distinctly unflattering.

The final night came when Madame, wearing her night turban and flowing négligé, entered my room without even knocking, to inform me she had had enough of me to last a lifetime, that I had ruined her life, her peace of mind and general health, and must pay what I owed her and be gone within twenty-four hours. When I protested that I could not find other accommodation at such short notice, Madame cursed me roundly and with such expressiveness that I discovered for the first time, by the colour and variety of her expressions, that her country of origin was in fact Russia rather than Poland.

I found a room with full board close by in Addison Road, Swiss Cottage, which looked much more inviting, with artistically arranged furniture, refectory table for diners, art drawings, lithographs and wood carvings. It was, apparently, unheated and the rooms struck chill. But the other boarders were artists, musicians, radio technicians, and I moved in gratefully at £3 15s for room and breakfast.

The landlady was a charming woman who rarely left her own attractive room, which appeared to be full of cats, lying upon the beds, around and under it. They were beautiful cats, many with their own pedigree and case-history: they included Persians, plain black cats, two pure white. One was called "Chocolate", and there were several terrifying Siamese. They had been trained to use the bathroom and lavatory, and they did, using the carpeted parts of the floor for preference. They also liked using the stairs for this purpose. To ascend or descend the staircase of that dimly-lit three-storey house was a nightmare resulting in a frequent outbreak of hysteria among the other boarders. One night we called a meeting of over-wrought paying-guests and presented a written petition to the landlady's distinguished-looking husband, who was something at the BBC.

We were told next day that Madame's whole object in undertaking the unrewarding task of running a boarding-house was to provide comfortable accommodation for her cats. As for our protests about the singular smell pervading all three storeys, Madame felt we were not only over-sensitive but inconsiderate as well.

I moved again, this time to a bare clean room at Chalk Farm. It was guaranteed mouse-free and had its own bathroom, in a cubicle in the corridor below. It had to be locked each time after use, as otherwise strangers could enter the front door and take a bath in it.

One night a skinny little mouse sprang out of my sheets just as

I was about to get into them. I spent the night in the armchair, under the leather coat, occasionally waking to throw shoes at the wall to try and frighten the mice away.

I thought of my tiny, freezing little room in the first hotel where I stayed on Tyneside. All the other boarders complained about the beetles. Me, I never minded a little thing like beetles.

Fleet Street, though, was not what I expected. I thought I should meet people who knew the truth about the important things, especially about politics and the two last wars and many more things. I had learned so much in the police courts on Tyneside, and now Fleet Street was going to fill me in on the rest. And when I knew the truth I should find an absolute to help me judge myself and others. I felt it would be simple then to make up my mind on all kinds of problems.

Then I should know how a woman could make her way alone in the world and still remain a woman. I mean, without doing something so mad as to try and kill herself or as stupid as crawling to a marriage bureau with her five guineas or whatever it was that you needed simply because you didn't feel able to take responsibility for yourself.

I should find out the answer to difficult questions like why my grandparents had run away from Russia; and why they and their children became so intolerant of each other, so that it had been like having a war on every day.

How lucky I was to be still young, earning enough to live on, just like a man, and how lucky to be a London girl reporter in 1945, because now I was so close to getting all my questions answered.

Later that year I went round the countryside in fast cars, to follow Winston Churchill on his election tour. I was running in and out of the lobby of the House of Commons as though it were my local milk bar, and taking a fast verbatim shorthand note when the men gathered to declare a gasworkers' strike, and a bus and railway strike or an electricians', one and so on. Afterwards I had to help in the search for the murderers Neville Heath and Haigh and Christie, and I stood on draughty street corners, talking it all over with the boys. I sat through week-long breach of promise cases in the High Court, and dog shows and cat shows. I chatted to Mrs Eleanor Roosevelt and Mary Pickford and later Nina Krushcheva as though I'd known them all my life. I felt I was right at the centre of things. Even the lonely-heart girls from Grove End Gardens envied me a little, though not too much because they believed that marriage was the only real fulfilment for a woman, and everything else, no matter what, was just a sort of compensation or making the best or it. I almost admired them for their wholeheartedness about this. Then this must be a sort of truth, surely, and I filed it away in my mind, so to speak, to set against the larger ones when I found them.

But I didn't find them. And though the pace kept quickening for us and the news got hotter every day, with the Lynskey tribunal, the Berlin air lift, and so on, I could feel myself and all my journalist colleagues changing. There was a sort of panic in the air. But what there was to panic about, none of us could say.

We were all earning more money than we'd ever hoped or dreamed about. In Newcastle I'd gone to an all-time high of £7 10s a week, with about £2 a week expenses. Now we earned £15 a week, then £20, then £30, £40 and £50, and more. The expenses were often so high that if you were smart enough you could practically live on them, and let your salary stay in the bank. Now I was often going into a restaurant and spending 10/- on a meal. I was comparatively rich. We all were. And yet we felt every day, more and more insecure, and it began to spoil our relationships. I would say to my friend Norman, "What a rotten writer Jack is". I felt certain Jack was saying the same about my stuff. All the old loyalties were breaking down.

CHAPTER XX

BACK AGAIN AMONG THE GERMANS

I MOVED INTO a German refugee boarding-house close to Swiss Cottage station. The cooking was German, so was the conversation and the total efficiency. Sometimes, though, a crisis blew up.

Herr Professor B., who was shy and modest and did not normally converse with anyone except for the obligatory "Morgen!", accompanied by a little bow, was heard by all of us to ask the landlady if by mistake she had given him margarine with his breakfast, instead of butter.

For the first time, the perfect order of our house was seen to crack with a mighty explosion. We sat and sat, but no breakfast came. The Frau Doktor, as she had once been in Mannheim, was in the kitchen, having hysterics. She was deeply hurt, we were informed, in her feelings. It was not the allegation itself, though that was serious enough, since if there were any truth in the Professor's accusation it could be a matter for the police at a time like this, with food rationing, especially of butter, down to its all-time lowest level, for which, it should be remembered, the Labour Government was now to blame and not Madame herself, who, sobbing bitterly, could be heard from behind the kitchen door, calling upon all to witness that never, never could she be guilty of so heinous a crime as to rob the Professor of his legal, infinitesimal butter ration. No, it was not the accusation that hurt, it was the lack of trust.

I left this establishment a few weeks later, not because I wanted to do so, although it was slightly more expensive than I could afford to pay, but because Madame did not like my entertaining a young Polish refugee lawyer in my room. It was quite true, as

Madame alleged, that we were indulging in illicit behaviour strictly forbidden by large printed notices on the walls of every room. That is to say, I was cooking for him—he was the tallest, skinniest, hungriest Pole I'd ever seen—a small tin of curry over a gas-ring, which was not intended by the Management for this purpose.

The Frau Doktor, in her accusation, implied that such illicit behaviour could well lead to other kinds of improper conduct in her opinion, and that her timely intervention might well have saved me from indiscretions which could only lead to regret even for a woman working, as she said she knew I did, in a profession not specifically noted for discretion. By this, the Frau Doktor meant that she thought Fleet Street was a place altogether too bohemian for her establishment, quite apart from the fact that it often made me late for meals.

I was, so to speak, on the road again, looking for just a room, oh, for a clean, warm, cheap room of my own!

In those days it was easier . . . as even my, formerly, lonely-heart cousins from Grove End Gardens were finding . . . to find a husband than to find a clean, warm, cheap room. As Cousin Roz kept saying to me in her downright way, "You ought to find yourself a decent flat and then it'll be a cinch to find a husband." Yes but where?

I was glad when I was sent on an assignment to Germany. There, surely, I would find out some absolute truth. About us humans.

Berlin was a mass of grey ruins in the rain, and it took several days to get used to the smell of dead bodies still lying under the mountains of rubble. Our hotel near the Am Zoo station seemed to be one of the few buildings still intact.

Sefton Delmer and Ian Colvin and Willie Forrest and Larry Solon sipped brandies and sat about in dusty armchairs. Sometimes they got up and mailed long dispatches to their papers. I

listened to long conversations about Germany, which was something I seemed to have been doing all my life.

Everyone in our press hotel left a cigarette beside his plate as a
tip for the waiters. I watched how they picked up each cigarette
as though it were a treasure and wrapped it carefully away. I kept
leaving more and more cigarettes about, and I felt guilty about it
too and somehow ashamed for some reason.

One day I took some English children, the family of the Control
Commissioner, and we played games and took photographs on
Hitler's broken balcony in the Wilhelmstrasse where he used to
make his speeches, until some Russian soldiers came and told us it
was not safe to play there.

One evening I took a taxi to an address given me by Fraülein
Pinkas from Metal Supplies, who had asked me to find out what
had happened to her old school headmistress whom she loved
very much. There was no electric light at night in the suburbs,
but with the driver's torch we managed to find the block of
flats and it was still standing. I started to climb the stairs, and then
my torch failed. In that total blackness it was impossible to see
even what sort of place it was. I was a little afraid then. How
would I ever get down again? There were holes everywhere, and
part of the banisters was missing.

I started to shout in my English-accented German, and to call
out the name of the old lady. My voice echoed fearfully through
the building. After a time I could hear footsteps and a door being
unbolted. She was very nervous of me, until I told her I came from
England, with a message from her old pupil, Ella Pinkas. I felt
very pleased to have found the right one. She had a torch and she
led me into her flat. I saw tall rooms, rather empty in the German
style, but they had once been elegant. She was wrapped in shawls
and seemed emotional and highly-strung. I handed over the
presents I had brought, a tin of coffee and some packets of
cigarettes. She burst into tears.

I went about Berlin and I felt more and more sorry for the Germans. And I felt there was something wrong with this feeling of mine, and wondered what it was.

Then one day on the Kurfurstendamm, or what remained of it, I saw from a little distance a very tall, handsome German officer still in his army uniform. He was slumped on a bench in the street with his profile towards me. As I passed he turned full face, and I saw that he had been, as I thought, extremely good-looking. But both eyes had been shot away, and nothing had been done to cover up the two bloody, gaping holes. I put a packet of cigarettes into his hand and walked on very quickly, and then I realised what was wrong with me. I had come upon a truth of sorts and it was about myself. I was sentimental and timid. I did not like the sight of blood, so the easiest thing was to look down at the man's hands and put cigarettes there, in order the quicker to forget the sight of the eye sockets.

When I got back to the Am Zoo press camp, there was a woman colleague there named Monica from *Reynolds News* and she was haranguing the men in their armchairs, saying that it was disgusting because we British were starving the Germans. She had been walking over the broken town looking for hungry German children so that she could give them her sweet ration. The other journalists listened silently and some of them smiled. I admired her for having the courage to be unpopular. I knew that I could never do this. I should always say to them "yes, yes, you are right", because for me it was more important to have them like me. So I decided that perhaps after all I was no better than the lonely-heart girls Lily and Roz and the rest. And marriage, it seemed, might after all be all I was fit for.

In Germany I always kept company with the Red Army, just as in the old days at Reuters I had sought out Misha Basharin for the midnight tea-break. I still felt comfortable only with the Russians. I could not even though I tried, see them as my journalist friends did, as child rapists or bullies. And I knew this was not because I had any political convictions about them but simply because to me they were familiar and homely and a little bit mad as all the Izvozchiks had been. They couldn't hold a knife and fork properly either, and sucked their sugar loudly as the glass of tea went down, before belching comfortably.

Above all, they were eccentric and dotty just like the English, reminding me once again that somewhere, somehow along the line there must have been a common origin.

CHAPTER XXI

BUT THE ENGLISH ARE POTTY TOO

RETURNING FROM GERMANY, I moved for a blissful few weeks into the Hampstead Towers Hotel in Ennerdale Road which, at six guineas a week, was the most lush and expensive I had ever known. We sat at little separate tables in the dining-room, each with our private pot of marmalade and vitamin tablets. There were two generals, a Polish admiral, an air marshal, a barrister, three doctors and an Indian Rajah in parma violet turban.

Next to me sat an apparently unmarried lady in green velvet corduroy jacket. "Theresa", said the green velvet lady, "you have brought me enough pudding for a mouse." She looked at Theresa with big, hungry eyes.

"Hev aye, moddom?" said Theresa, putting another slice of delicious treacle sponge in front of her.

We all watched each other's plates to see that we were getting a full six guineas' worth of the food rations, which were meagre enough.

I noticed that the green velvet lady always had a copy of the *Soviet News Weekly* propped against her water jug, though I never saw her turn a page or read a line. But the sight of this, together with the Polish admiral's wife's *Daily Worker* seemed proudly to defy the surrounding tables decorated with *The Times* and the *Daily Sketch*, my own employers.

Sometimes the proud, upright figure of the air marshal, his breast sagging under the weight of his medals, bent over the green velvet lady, sitting behind her Soviet defence.

"How interesting," said the air marshal, "dear me, how interesting. Is it in the Russian language?" Clearly, he had not noticed the words *Soviet Weekly* in big, black type.

I noticed that it was a habit of well-bred English gentlefolk, especially those among us now taking up residence in private hotels in Hampstead and Kensington after a long stint of duty with the Raj in India, to pretend to be a little blind or deaf.

"Yes, it is so very interesting," said the lady with the *Soviet Weekly*. "My deah"—she was addressing the air marshal's wife— "you simply must see it when I have finished it."

We were in Britain still in the middle of our war-time friendship with the Soviet Union.

Sometimes the generals with their straight ramrod backs would stop to chat with me. "Such a gallant little paper, the *Daily Sketch*," said the general one day. I was surprised to be noticed, because the general's eyes never actually focussed on anything inside a room but were always seeing some remote, I thought, horizon.

"Your life must be so interesting," said the general. He asked what thrilling assignment was being prepared for me this day.

I was down on the news schedule to cover a meeting of the Poetry Society near Marble Arch. Poetry was suddenly news, because *Picture Post* had done a big article about it, with photographs, and so I got the "follow-up" to do.

Our photographer and I were shown into the committee rooms where the three poets, chosen for the evening's business, and one "reader", in a low-cut, floral gown, sipped sherry. They were discussing Byron. The Society's secretary, who was wearing a New-Look, long-skirted suit in green, came up to us and said, "I am not at all anti-traditionalist, you know."

I said, "I'm so glad."

She introduced me to the poets. "This is our rising young poet."

This one had a very white face behind thick tortoiseshell glasses and a strong Yorkshire accent.

"I find him so virile," she added.

Our photographer kept close to me as we were shown into a large room where about thirty people were sitting in rows on hard chairs. There was a dim light from candle-shaped globes and a big notice "no smoking". One woman wore a long black velvet cloak. The chosen poets took seats in the front row because they knew the "reader" was going to read out their work. Tony walked up and down the rows with his camera, and everyone shrank away modestly. The woman in the floral gown started reading the poems, though it must have been difficult in that dim light. The poems included lines about the black thorn and love. One was called "On being dead". When the front row had their poems read, the authors smiled and blushed and everyone clapped.

It went on for an hour. Then the chairman made a speech. He said he had never before heard poems read "so lovingly".

But it was not only poetry of the more portentous kind that the British people loved. As life steadily became, or looked like becoming, more normal, as green grass and purple and yellow weeds were torn out of the bomb craters in the streets and replaced by ugly office blocks modelled on the American style, I was finding that the people round me, albeit strangers, were just as fascinating as my own family once had been.

War-time photographs of soldiers or politicians were now being replaced in the newspapers by those of cuddly dogs, cats, snakes, bears, or any other animals dear to English hearts. The Board of the Cat Fancy was soon re-constituted, dog-loving societies got on their feet again, and day after day I was dispatched, sulky and apprehensive, as I disliked cats and was mortally afraid of small dogs, to record the measurements, personality and appearance of the various prize-winners at the constantly recurring cat and dog shows.

Not that this passion for animals revealed all, or even very

much, about the British character. What it did prove to me was
how wrong nearly all generalisations were. True, I had met
Scotsmen who were not mean and Irishmen who did not drink;
I met Viennese who did not waltz and Welshmen who did not
sing; I met Jews who were not clever and Spaniards who were
cold; I met Frenchmen who had no taste and Swedes who were
always jolly; as well as Swiss who were not stodgy and Americans
who had no money. But, contrary to the usual generalisations,
the English people and the Russian ones were still, I was pleased
to find, the maddest, the most talkative and the most eccentric.
So were my Izvozchik family so different after all . . . from any of
these Anglo-Saxons?

Sometimes my investigations on these subjects led me into
trouble. At this time I had moved to my worst accommodation
yet, at Barons Court. Some journalist colleagues had decided to
buy a house, in which I was to have had a share. Then at the last
minute the plan fell through and we were all left stranded. My
new rented room was now so cheerless, icy, that more than ever
I fled, as so many Londoners did in those days, to the cafés and
restaurants in order to get warm enough after the day's work to
go to bed.

Therefore I had many adventures. Like many plain girls who
have been reared to believe that they could never, easily, appeal
to men, I had, I think, an ingratiating, "shmoozy" manner which
often promised more than it was ever likely or willing to fulfil.
Especially with men.

I couldn't resist the novelty of any fresh encounter in a café,
if it were a new nationality like Turk or Greek that I had not met
before. I just couldn't let well alone. After losing my room in the
German boarding-house at Swiss Cottage while entertaining the
thin, thin Polish lawyer to my inexperienced curry, I then nearly
lost my life by almost being strangled in a fight with a very
nearly overwhelming Czech colonel in a taxi-cab. True, it made

a good story to tell next day. And my business was nothing if not telling stories. I had, it seemed, almost without knowing it, become a rather jolly girl who took nothing seriously, except of course the business of writing stories for the paper, the while pursuing the constant fascinating difference between one foreign national and another.

Then something happened which was to keep me out of the cafés and coffee-houses, as they were then, for quite some years.

One spring evening, in the Finchley Road, I heard the familiar voices of Russian women talking. "Nu, harasho, nam para . . ." (All right, it's time to go).

It seemed so long since I'd heard my loved language . . . not since Captain Ivanov on Tyneside and the mysterious Russian businessman who had taken me to the pictures. To me, as always, it was the eternal magnet, which would lead me, surely, back to Father, where I would be seven years old again, upon his knees, listening.

The two women separated, and one went into a nearby café and sat down at a little table and ordered coffee. I followed her and sat down opposite her.

CHAPTER XXII

ESTHER

HER NAME WAS Esther Haham. She had been a medical student at Kiev University when Lenin came to final power, and later, in 1919, she fled via Bucarest to Vienna to rejoin her parents who had managed to escape there from their home in Ekaterinburg.

As one of the intellectuals of that time, Esther never wanted to flee, never wanted to leave Russia. But her father, a wealthy jeweller, was in some danger, and to her the family was the most important thing. Her mother had been a dentist, practising at home, for it had been then the normal thing for educated Russian women to have a profession or job. Earlier, at the age of forty-one, Esther's father had decided to go to university and take a degree.

They were educated Russians who called themselves Jews. They were as far removed from the Izvozchiks, for example, as educated people could be from a primitive tribe. Every member of her family belonged to a profession: they were lawyers or doctors; they had been to universities; they were free to live in Moscow or Leningrad or wherever they liked. They also called themselves Zionists, but they could not speak or understand a word of Hebrew or Yiddish.

During and after the First World War Austrian prisoners-of-war had been interned near her home, and Esther and her sister Lucia had made friends with several of these soldiers, who were allowed to visit families from time to time. One of them, a Viennese lawyer named Michael Grün, later became her husband, when her family took refuge in Vienna.

After the Anschluss in 1938, Esther and her schoolboy son

George were helped by an English Protestant priest to escape and come to London, where he gave them a home and had George sent to Winchester College. Later he went to Cambridge University.

Michael refused to leave Vienna as long as he could help any Jews to escape abroad. He was arrested by the Gestapo, and sent to the concentration camp of Theresienstadt.

So Esther was still hopeful that he might be still alive. Theresienstadt was known to be the "model" concentration camp, that is to say, it was then believed that prisoners at the camp were not tortured or put in gas ovens. The evidence for this had been provided by visitors who had been allowed to inspect the camp.

But now Esther was becoming anxious. Every day the International Red Cross were supplying lists of names of survivors and every day there was hope that Michael's name might be among them, but it never was.

She was still waiting for news when I met her, and we sat and talked. She was shocked at the way I spoke Russian, almost without grammar or grace. It was decided that, until the news came through that Michael was safe, she would give me lessons in grammar and we would study literature and poetry and art, all in the Russian language.

So we began long abstract discussions in Russian which lasted for hours at a time. And so began a long friendship which endured for twenty years and had a lasting influence on me.

I stopped going to the cafés to look for "adventures". I lost interest in the Poles, the Czechs and all the others. Instead I was put through a course of Tolstoy, Turgenev, Dostoyevsky, Goncharov, Gogol, Gorki and Chekhov, with plays and poems of Pushkin and Lermontov, to be learned by heart. It was the end of the jolly girl. Now, when the telephone rang, I did not even bother to answer it.

I had never known anyone like Esther, who could show me

how to lose myself in the contemplation of abstractions or in philosophy. Now it was more interesting to talk about love than to look for it. She had a power of concentration which I had rarely found in English life, and this she could focus on any job in hand, even upon trivia like making an omelette or a bowl of "mousak". Slowly and painfully, I felt I was being given what an ordinary schooling had failed to give, the power to think.

Her very integrity sometimes made her unlovable. When I made mistakes, which was often, she regarded me with contempt. "You are superficial," she cried at such times, "you are English in your way of study. Superficial!" Or if I were tired she could barely understand it. "Tired? How can anyone be tired when there is a job to be done? Ah, you English, you English, you are always tired." She reminded me of Dr Margolin. In fact, she had known him; they had had the same schooling, the same friends. When I made a mistake in grammar, her voice rose to a high wail: "Olga, oh Olga, Vwy menya ubivayete, ya stradayu"—you are killing me, how I suffer.

No wonder the neighbours used to bang on the walls in wonderment or fear at all the noise. I lived now in a tiny flat in Albany Street near Regent's Park.

At last the Red Cross issued their final lists of names. There was no hope and never had been. Theresienstadt camp had been no different from the others. But they had other family news for her. Her elderly mother, her sister Lucia, with her husband, and their little boy had been trapped in Sofia, where they lived. One day the SS came and made them all march to the big square, where all were shot.

So for a little while—it lasted about a month—our talks on life and love and philosophy were interrupted. Next time I went to see her the dark head of Esther had turned completely grey.

CHAPTER XXIII

LILY WEDDED

LIFE DOES, HOWEVER, usually give people what they most want. Many people don't recognise it, when given, so it is lost to them anyway.

This was not the case, however, with the lonely-heart girls of Grove End Gardens. Three of the group had now got their hearts' desire. Rozlie was already married to a nice Viennese who designed confectionery for the Queen, Rita married the composer Hans May, and, though Jane, Kitty, Anne and many more were still as they were, even Lily won through in the end. Everyone was agreed upon it; if anyone deserved to be married, Lily did.

Rozlie wanted everyone to be present when Lily told how she did it, to avoid repetition. But as each guest arrived Lily began again at the beginning. "He was standing on his own. I was dancing with this ghastly man. I was in agony in case he wasn't alone and the Other Woman was in the lav or something. I made up my mind there and then. This one's mine. I went up and stared deeply into his eyes."

"Like a snake," said Jane, giggling.

"Let her get on with it," said Rozlie. "There's lots more."

Kitty sniffed. "I'd die rather than ask a man . . ." Kitty was a bit gloomy. She'd just been on a visit to America, where everyone assured her she would find a husband immediately. And now she was back with us, still without one.

"I think I'll go and make the tea," said Aunt Sally. She was smiling, though. It was a great relief to her as well as to all of us that Lily was suited at last.

"Aunty Sal," shouted Lily after her, "nothing obscene I promise. I'm saving the erotic bits for later."

"Girls!" Lily rushed on, "it took me all day to put my eyes on. Bloody hard work . . . those green and silver lids take *hours*. And then each eyelash. Separately. How will I do it after we're married? I mean, if Don insists. He said that's why he hadn't married before. He's seen how they let themselves go—you know, afterwards. So I had to promise. All those eyelashes. My God!"

Rozlie said to hurry up and get to the juicy part. "Paul will be home soon. I don't want him disillusioned with all your technical details."

Lily was describing the special uplift bra she'd had on. Jane wanted the address of the shop, the price, measurements, etc.

"You know, girls, what really did the trick," said Lily. "To think all the years I've wasted, using the wrong technique. I met this Irish woman on the 53A bus. She was trying to sell me a bunch of heather or something. So I told her I'd just met the right man. And she said 'You have to be melting always. Be melting, my dear,' she said. 'I was cocky and I lost mine'."

"Oh do get on with it!" said Rozlie.

Lily said it was to be a slap-up affair. "At that swank place in Upper Berkeley Street where all the bloody rich Jews get married. I went and registered. When I had to write Lily B. . . . Spinster, a cold shiver went up my spine; think of being *that* unutterable thing."

Mother was giving the slap-up do. "I've waited long enough for it, don't you agree, girls?" Meanwhile Mother was acting as chaperone for their more tender moments together.

"I don't want to frighten him, you see," said Lily. "If anything goes wrong now, it would kill me. So I shan't show him, you know, anything new. Just in case."

Don was a night-hire driver. He'd saved and bought a nice little house for his mother, who had died before they could move in. "Anyway, experiments are out," Lily said. "Poor Don just had a car accident and hurt his back."

Aunt Sally was pouring the tea. "You've no shame, Lily." In fact, poor Lily was on the verge of nervous collapse. Now the six weeks of sleepless nights and anxiety about getting Don to the point were over, she could neither sit, lie nor sleep. A doctor was keeping her heavily dosed with barbituric opiates.

"I'm going to wear all snow-white," she said. "You know girls, I've discovered that honesty pays off. I've told Don all about my past, and all the details, and he was simply fascinated. He kept on asking for more."

Lily broke down under the marriage canopy, the "Chuppah". The crowded, rather beautiful and exclusive synagogue at Upper Berkeley Street, seven guineas extra, as well as the Rabbi with an American accent, were frozen quite immobile for about five or six minutes while Lily sobbed.

We all stiffened in our seats. Lily began touchingly enough with a little sniff. Suddenly a torrent of sobbing began and it was clear that, though Lily was trying to control her emotion, the effort was too much for her. In the end the Rabbi took her in his arms, the white net off-the-shoulder gown spangled with tiny gold stars and the white and silver crown and all, and comforted her. It happened while she was signing her name in the book after the ceremony while standing still under the canopy, and a ray of sunshine shone down on the radiant white figure. It was all suddenly too much, and when the couple finally left several minutes late, to the strains of here-comes-the-bride, Lily's elaborate make-up was gone forever.

We were all rather emotionally over-strung, in fact. All her friends were there, Jew and Gentile, young and old, male and female, former boy friends and girl friends whom she had made haphazardly everywhere; and they clearly all loved her so much that they were even ready to forgive her the white gown and gold stars and all the other unsuitable decoration. They even seemed pleased about it, breathing an admiring "oh" at her entrance, for all felt this was certainly Lily's Day, her moment of triumph.

Afterwards there was a red-coated toastmaster, five guineas extra, and Lily wore herself out trying to make all the single boys and girls present pair off together.

It was a triumph, too, of mind over matter. For Lily with her spoiled make-up and her strikingly plain looks was no beauty even in youth. But because she was pure in heart and so radiant with happiness, everyone seemed to suffer a trick of eyesight. We all kept yelling in chorus over and over that she looked gorgeous, wonderful, beautiful, glamorous, heavenly, and all of us, men as well as women, really meant it. We were caught up somehow in her own belief that, on that day anyway, she was beautiful.

Lily had gone to endless trouble to invite a "boy" for each of us. She was not so blinded by her own happiness, which had been achieved so suddenly and unexpectedly, that she could forget that there were still a large number of us "Girls", her own friends included, who were not and did not look like being very quickly "fixed-up". There was even a middle-aged single male guest specially invited for Aunt Sally, who went home early, not pleased. Lily, in going-away dress, pleaded—in vain.

After Lily's marriage the lonely-hearts club broke up. There was no need now for Friday night talks on strategy or progress reports. Everyone was safely married—that is, except Jane and Aunt Sally and Anne and Kitty and me.

We did meet again, though, at the Grove End Gardens flat some three years later. Looking round at us all to see what fulfilment, or its opposite, had done to us, I could see little change except that we were older. Our only real feature in common was, as the Bible calls it, our barrenness.

Lily, however, still thought that a baby could happen to her, which showed that Lily had not changed. Marriage, I was pleased to see, had in no way reduced her optimisim or gaiety.

Cousin Roz's husband Paul cooked our dinner, so this was one big change. We had never before eaten so deliciously. Paul seemed aghast at the conversation, as well he might be.

Roz was elegant as ever in tweed dress with brown velvet lapels and cuffs. Uncle Abe's daughter Jane, more plumply smooth, more blonde than ever, was curled in exhaustion in Roz's favourite chair. Roz, clearly, didn't like this. It was her best chair, for one thing, and for another she didn't think Jane had a right to look exhausted, since Jane didn't work while Roz did, in her little fancy millinery business off Baker Street, trying to persuade difficult customers that they looked marvellous in her hats.

Aunt Sally, as always, supplied a sort of negative goodwill which was, clearly, not going to do anybody any good, but nevertheless had a lifetime of earnest trying behind it. Somehow the lack of cosmetics on her face made her seem younger in comparison with us, whose paint and powder cruelly accentuated each line and wrinkle.

I sipped Paul's coffee and, in a sudden mood of clear-sightedness brought on by this meeting after all the years between, saw myself as plainly as I saw them. I knew all too well how I looked, with my eternal schoolgirl outfit crowned with dusty beret from which strands of my long-haired bun kept escaping. A button was missing from the shiny black jacket I wore. Below this a black jumper was held together by two—I fervently hoped—invisible gold safety-pins which in turn protected a faded candy-striped blouse, breast-tight from its twelve years' wearing. In fact, I was my Father's daughter still. I was the daughter of that Izzy Izvoz-chik who had, especially during his "rich" period, affected a cap and muffler in order more closely to identify with the truly British working class.

Lily looked a treat, slim and well-groomed. The slimness, we learned, was due to a recent attack of gastric influenza.

Jane wanted to talk about necromania. Lily too. "Come on you," said Roz to me, "you've seen the murderer Christie in court. Tell us the details."

I tried doing this, rather loudly, in order to be heard above the din. Jane had a better account than mine, obtained from a Sunday paper.

Lily was saying she'd discussed the whole thing with her doctor. "Do you know what he said," Lily went on. "It is passivity the murderer craves."

After some discussion Sally wanted the subject changed, but was overruled. At last we all got tired of Mr Christie. Besides Lily, had a better story.

"You've got to listen," Lily said, "because it could happen to you or to anyone. It'll be a lesson to you all . . . never, never to lock the lavatory or bathroom door, no matter what."

Interruption came here from Roz, who said she never locked; Jane hardly ever locked; and Paul said he too didn't ever lock. Aunt Sally and I were not asked whether we locked or not, though as I was sitting next to Sally on the couch I thought I heard her murmur that she left the door wide open.

I ought perhaps to advise the gentle reader, if he has not already suspected something, not to read on here. But I am supposed to be writing my true story in this little book, so it's no use dodging the facts, or falsifying what has lain in my secret journal these many years.

The truth in this case was that Lily and her beloved had had a little tiff. Don went to the lavatory and locked the door. There followed a short interval, and no sound came from Don.

Lily, after a little time had elapsed, began to worry. This polite silence, which, as Jane interrupted to say, could have been interpreted by some people as mere good breeding, began to get on her nerves. Besides she was keen for a quick reconciliation.

She rattled on the locked door.

"Don," she said, "what are you doing?"

There was no reply. Don, obviously, was smoking. Another interval elapsed. Lily tried the door again and called out. No reply. She tried to peer through the keyhole, but was unable to catch a glimpse of Don in any position whatever. Something terrible, it suddenly occurred to the anxious Lily, must have happened to Don. He did not normally sulk as long as this.

Lily related how she then lay flat on her face and tried to look under the crack of the door, sniffing for smoke, flame or other disaster. Was Don on fire or had he fainted? Lily's imagination was beginning to work, fast. "My Don," she said, "in danger in the locked lavatory . . ."

Don was weak after a bout of the same gastric 'flu, and she began to realise that she ought not to have crossed him. In despair, she remembered their devoted neighbour Mr Wheeler.

Mr Wheeler's solid, capable, comforting figure arrived immediately, breathing helpfulness. Lily, who had not, she hoped, forgotten all the various ways of appealing to a man's gallantry, fell on his bosom, as she herself put it, imploring him to save her Don. Mr Wheeler kept his head and fetched a ladder, mounting to gaze at Don, or whatever remained of Don, through the lavatory window.

"We thought of breaking the window with a brick," said Lily, "but the glass would have fallen on poor Don."

Mr Wheeler took one peep through the window and seemed quite overcome. Don, he shouted down, sat crouched in a dead faint in the exact position Mr Wheeler had seen dead men crouch during his war-time days in the A.R.P. This gave Mr Wheeler a terrible turn. Lily comforted him as best she could, and when he

felt stronger he went next door to collect some tools. He then
returned with the contents of his workbox, including a cutting
tool, and having cut out the entire lavatory window he fed Lily's
newly-slim form through the window to the rescue. She unlocked
the door at last, but was helpless to lift her loved one from the
lavatory seat. Again Mr Wheeler came to the rescue and, gather-
ing up the prostrate Don, carried him to the bed while Lily
telephoned for assistance.

"It was only then," said Lily, who was clearly impressed by the
rapt attention with which we were following her tale, "that I
noticed the poor boy had got his knickers down. So while he was
still unconscious I pulled them up and Don was saved. Oh, it
was a terrible experience. Never, never, I beg you, ever lock your
door."

Roz said, "how awful for you. I never lock, nor Paul, do you,
Peppie?"

Roz got up and said it was time for tea and macaroons. Jane
shrank more deeply into Roz's favourite chair. "It is a great pity,"
said Roz—and there was all the early Izvozchik savagery in her
voice as she said it—"that *you*, Jane, can't do something for a
change. Sitting there, after doing nothing all day."

"You're the hostess," said Jane, "do it yourself. I'm not your
servant."

Some hissing and shouting followed. But Lily again came to
the rescue. *She* would do it, she said, she would make the tea
herself. For all of us.

I made a half-hearted move and raised myself as far as the arm
of the divan. However, all was soon calm again. I could hear faint
sounds from the kitchen where Roz was opening her heart to
Lily about the faults in the character of Uncle Abe's only daughter
Jane.

Later, as we took our lukewarm tea and ate macaroons, Lily
told us about Don's stomach, which was not strong.

Did she regret exchanging her earlier, more adventurous life for it? Lily said no, she had no regrets. "All that doesn't mean a thing to me now," said Lily. "You can call me a reformed tart if you like; I'm totally devoted to Don even if he has got a weak tum."

Late that night Lily and Jane saw me off from St John's Wood underground station. It was a send-off that caught the attention of all the male occupants of the tube train, which, as it was the last train of the night, remained stationary with doors wide open for several minutes.

Clinging to the open doors I prayed for them to close on the shrill voice and gestures of my companions, Lily and Jane.

"Don't forget" Lily was screaming to me, "N.Y.F. . . . N.Y.F. . . . Ha, ha, ha, ha!"

The passengers in that train could not know, of course, that these initials had the quite innocent interpretation of Nice Yiddisher Fellow—which Lily insisted was the only true basis for happiness. She wished all of us still unmarried "Girls", Aunt Sally included, an N.Y.F. with all the good kindness of her loving heart.

It was clear from the sniggers all round me that Londoners in that tube train saw a wholly other meaning in Lily's repeated calls and shouts from the platform. And when the train doors finally and all too slowly closed before my perspiring face and shut out the dreadful sounds, I did not have the courage to sit down.

CHAPTER XXIV

COLD WAR OF THE GIRL-REPORTER

THE PHYSICAL HARDSHIPS of being a reporter surprised me. I had not reckoned with vigils on street corners in the rain, teetering on high heels, bare-legged, owing to lack of clothing coupons and lack of sense, in the snow to attend the gasworkers' constantly recurring strikes, or the meat-market men's, or the busmen's stoppage.

Remembering George Thompson's advice to me to "specialise girl, for God's sake", I knew it had to get worse before it could get better; and with the advent of the Shinwell Winter in 1947 it did.

I was assigned to visit children's homes throughout England, Wales and Scotland in order to investigate the facts behind the recent Curtis report about neglected, unhappy children.

The Children's Home near Bridgend outside Cardiff was nice, with affectionate foster mothers and a stone-flagged kitchen with a roaring fire. The weather was turning cold, but it was still not too bad. Meeting the children, however, was a strange experience. They seemed, on the acquaintance of a day or two, somehow, gentler, handsomer, more lovable than ordinary "legitimate" children, but the worst thing was that when the time came to leave them they clung to one's arms or clothes, or the smaller ones clutched one round the legs. It was somehow alarming, all the more so because the foster parents in most cases were kindly and warm-hearted. They tried to explain to me that what the children wanted was something of their own, something that needn't be shared with all the others; so that when a visitor came they competed for attention, in the restrained, subdued way that life had imposed upon them. Each child tried with a sort of desperation to charm the visitor.

That November, as I worked my way northwards, the cold had become intense by the time I had finished touring the Midlands. On the radio Mr Emmanuel Shinwell, Minister of Fuel and Power in the Labour Government, was protesting that it wasn't his fault that both light and heat would have to be rationed. The snow in the streets froze hard, layer on layer of it. In the hotels we dined on cold soup and cold meat, and drank lukewarm coffee by candlelight. Guests were asked kindly not to take a bath, or the bathroom would have to be locked. And the weather in the streets got colder.

My orders were to take the train from Leicester to Edinburgh to investigate if the Scots, who had a separate children's and health department, were better at caring for children than we were.

Inside the unheated railway carriages passengers sat blue-lipped, stone-faced with the cold. Some wrapped newspapers round their legs, but it proved impossible to keep any sort of body heat, for few had any warm clothing, which was still strictly rationed. It was a nightmare journey: the train kept stopping through lack of coal; there was no dining-car; and piled snow and ice on the line made progress slower still. We could not see out of the windows, which were thickly laced with ice and snow.

Edinburgh was a great relief. The Scots had coal and better weather, and cosy hotel maids who brought hot towels and ran hot baths. I stayed in bed at the North British Hotel nursing a hacking cough, and it was all like a dream of unbelievable comfort. I longed to stay, at least for a week. Could I spin out my Curtis investigation report on Scotland for as long as that? I took some aspirins and went to sleep. About 10.30 that night the news editor telephoned from London. There was a village in Staffordshire which had been cut off by snowdrifts for about a week. No one could get through to the villagers, who'd had no bread, no milk, no newspapers, and there were some cottages which could not even open their front doors for the high-piled snow. Hand-trained as I once had been by Herr Doktor Mayer, I knew better than to argue with the boss. "How will I get through?" I said hoarsely, "if the baker and the milkman can't manage it?"

"Look, I'm doing you a favour," said news editor Harold Dickson, "I'm putting you on the story of a lifetime. Can ye no go by horseback?"

He was a Glasgow man himself. A real news-hawk, madly keen. "I want a real colour story; pull all the stops out and give it all you've got. If ye can not get a horse, lass, you'd best go on foot, and take a sack with loaves of bread and cigarettes. Och, man, what a story!"

No, he wasn't getting me mixed up with anyone else. To Fleet Street news editors, we were all men; well, that was the whole point, wasn't it? That's why I'd wanted to be a reporter in the first place.

A taxi took me and a local photographer to within three miles of the trapped village. He said we'd never make it, but we did, wading almost up to our waists right up to the cottage doors. The only things which didn't survive were the sacks of cigarettes and bread; they got soaked by the snow, which started to come down again then.

I got pleurisy after that, and the paper never used the story because they couldn't get the picture of me up to my neck in snow back to London in time for the first edition, as the trains were not running owing to lack of coal.

Then, as the fifties began, everything started to change, to warm up. Sweets were still rationed, but foreign restaurants were opening up, offering food the like of which had not been seen by us since war began. Jugoslavia was sending sausage and salami, the Czechs too; the French sent cheese; the Poles sent eggs, the

Dutch butter; and now every day that passed brought us a better, easier life. My life was getting better too, in other ways. . . .

I was now nearly thirty-seven. I could no longer hope for love, let alone a marriage. Certainly not in Britain. The British have never cared much for older women, and many Englishmen, including, oddly enough, many English doctors, have always had a vague notion that for women the menopause, or what is better known to them as "a funny time", began round about the age of forty. This might well be why Englishwomen over twenty-one tended to look and to feel discouraged, in comparison with the women of other nationalities.

The alternative, of course, was always open, namely, to lead a life of "gallantry" just like a man, a course recommended by many progressive women like Brigid Brophy and Miss Simone de Beauvoir. My own experience led me to believe that this was no solution to the dilemma of being a lone woman living alone. For a woman, it seemed to me, a life of gallantry contained pleasures almost imperceptible and pains which included the chief one of all, namely, that pleasure of any degree changed any woman from gallantry to being un-gallant awfully quickly.

Russians, I always found, were less fussy over this problem of age. This might be due to the fact that on the whole Russian women were less likely to have a "funny time" at any age whatever, but also because, when obvious attractions were gone, the Russian man could still enjoy, as he liked to call it, her Russian soul.

However, that might be, I was not expecting, at thirty-seven, to find any personal happiness. I spent my days and nights, when not actually up in an aeroplane, swapping not very good stories with the boys while standing at the cheerless, ugly, Fleet Street bars, longing for a nice sit-down and a hot cup of tea but realising now, all too painfully, that journalism could never ever be done sitting down.

Nevertheless, I still thought about love. For one thing, it was a

subject never very far from the news editor's or features editor's
news schedule. Often, in fact, in the absence of any resounding
murder-story, love was our only business. For this reason I was
sent, more often than not, to interview the great writers, in the
hope that they would say something interesting or new upon this
question.

These were among my favourite assignments, though women
writers sometimes made me nervous. There was nearly always
a good tea, with home-made jam and a blessed sit-down by a
warm fire. Sometimes there were even my favourite cucumber
sandwiches.

Some, of course, were kind and considerate and even tender,
like Somerset Maugham and J. B. Priestley and Charles Morgan,
who all had the tact to worry in case you'd had nothing to eat or
drink; or perhaps you were just tired out after being flogged to
death by unthinking news editors, and so on. This was restful,
even inspiring. The late Mr Maugham, for example, never forgot
to write and thank you for whatever you wrote about him. In
fact, with him the preliminaries always took such a long time that
by the time you were ready to get out the pen and little notebook, with your feet up on a velvet stool and a whisky in your
hand, it was nearly too late to get the interview. Mr Maugham,
like Mr Priestley, was magnanimously interested in your health,
your experiences, and how much they paid or under-paid you.
So you went away from interviews like these feeling that, give
or take a few weeks' freedom or so, you too could easily write a
book like *The Good Companions* or *Cakes & Ale*.

Visits to women writers were not so comforting. There was
the disconcerting feeling that Miss Edna O'Brien or Miss Doris
Lessing or even the beautiful and brilliant Drabble sisters might
need one day to put some luckless woman reporter like me into a
book. Especially as Miss O'Brien said she didn't get out much or
meet many people. It made me cringe a bit, facing, as boldly as I

could, these and many more immensely talented lady writers, to know that their acute observation could hardly have missed the evidence of a misspent life; namely, that the reporter's shoes had not been cleaned for ages, that her hair had a coquettish untidiness suited to a much younger woman, and that her girl-reporter's manner—voice teetering a little unsteadily on some high notes —was always hotly, over hotly, eager to please and to reassure that her traffic with the said lady-writer was intended only to praise and enrich and be generally good for sales.

All this was of course unfair and unjust and over-womanly, but it was typical of the self-consciousness with which not only I, but most of my men and women colleagues too, half-educated, some of them, just as I was, went about our business.

Then began the era known as "digging" for news. And soon I was back on that well-worn royal trail.

Our new editor, the late Bert Gunn, wanted me to do five articles on the royal children, Prince Charles, aged five and Princess Anne, all about their food and behaviour and little sayings in the nursery, which had now moved, with the death of the King, to Buckingham Palace.

Mr Gunn was a tall, impressive man who, I knew as we all did, liked to be at least equally impressed by our drive and efficiency. "You know what I want," said Mr Gunn (who is father of the poet Thom Gunn). It was a statement, not a question. Alas, I knew only too well. He shook my hand, and then kissed my cheek in a friendly way. It was not only a mark of esteem but was meant also to set the seal on the importance of this assignment. But I needed no kissing to be forewarned of the grinding ordeal before me.

First, I should have "to go through the motions", as we called it in our jargon. Ring Buckingham Palace and ask to see Commander Colville or his assistant. Make an appointment to call. I should be received most kindly and told "You know the rules; we can't tell you anything". Then you put down on your expense sheet for a 5s taxi ride to Buck House, and 5 bob back. And then the real work began.

My usual way of starting—to keep up my reputation for being the biggest moaner in the business—and to relieve the "nerves", was to put my head down on my desk and sob a little. Then the chaps came.

"What's the matter?" asked Norman Hare, who was always tender-hearted.

"I think she's having a baby," said Jack Lewis. "I recognise the noises, the bodily spasms. My wife was like that with her third."

Sidney Butt, the news editor, and Bert Pack, the copy-taster, came to take a look at me.

"She's got the royal children", Jack said. "Five articles with all the gen."

"Poor kid," said Sidney, a sympathetic man.

"Poor kid," said Bert.

I began to feel better. I'd just remembered Cousin Roz of the one-time lonely-heart girls from St John's Wood. Only a week earlier I had been invited to dine with her and Jane Davis and Aunt Sally and all. And Roz's husband Paul had told us all about his recent visits to Buckingham Palace and Clarence House, where he discussed all the chocolates and cakes and sweets which the royal households would like. And Paul had mentioned that there was a charming new housekeeper who had cooked for the Queen at the Palace, and had now moved to Clarence House to cook for the Queen Mother and Princess Margaret. And only this very week, heaven be praised, the royal children were staying with their Grandmother at Clarence House.

It was the done thing in those days to lie and trick and deceive if you had to do so, in order to get the "copy".

I invited Mrs Alma McKee to dinner, presenting myself as a

friend of her friend Paul. I said I was a Canadian housewife (Canada seemed a nice, safe long way away, so I thought she'd feel more comfortable), and my husband worked for a newspaper. As she was from Stockholm herself, she didn't even spot that my accent was a bit odd even for a Canadian.

I couldn't say that what I got amounted to much, except a few nursery sayings, and the daily menu, which included grilled grapefruit for breakfast as Prince Charles always liked it. But the editor, when he saw the stuff said he was "happy".

That was my life now, to keep him and a whole string of subsequent editors happy.

The previous year had seen an outbreak of strikes and calls for action at excited trade union meetings. We marched once in a great body to the union meeting and declared the strike was on. We ate sandwiches, listened to speeches, sang "Knees up Mother Brown", and then went home, uneasy, in a biting wind. It was nearly Christmas, time to think of buying presents.

Days went by, and we stood at street corners and in the cold, uncomfortable public bars, or took turns at picketing the entrance to Kemsley House along with the solitary, half-frozen policeman.

Of course we won. The proprietor, who was then Viscount Kemsley, gave in; our just demands would be met, all of them. The cold printing presses slowly warmed up, started to revolve again. But it was too late to save them.

Each one died in turn. Ours went first, the *Daily Sketch* and *Graphic*, but in the end we were the luckiest. Within twenty-four hours came news that Viscount Rothermere would take us over into his group, the Associated Newspapers. In a statement, we were told that he felt he could not allow the *Sketch*, which his uncle, Lord Northcliffe, had founded, die like that. We were not to know then, in 1952, that many more papers would also die before the decade was out. After that the *Sunday Graphic* failed, then the *Sunday Chronicle*, the *Sunday Empire News*. . . .

G

The street was getting narrower. That was the winter of 51/52, when the black smog came down.

We, who had been saved at the eleventh hour, moved from the crumbling Kemsley House in Gray's Inn Road, from the rats scuttling in the basement canteen and the dark sweating walls. It was just around the corner from where Karl Marx's daughter, the beautiful Eleanor, had lived with her lover more than fifty years earlier, until that block of flats where she lived No. 65, New Stone Buildings, Chancery Lane, had been destroyed by a bomb in 1940. Now we had shining, new offices on the corner of Carmelite Street overlooking the Thames, and, though I did not know it, my real reporting work was about to begin. All the rest up till now had been just an apprenticeship.

My next job was to chase the Duke of Windsor, which was much worse really, as it meant pretending, in bad French, to be anything else *but* a reporter, in order to get inside their new mill house near Paris. I was frightened to death with all the Duchess's dogs snapping at my heels, but the Duke took it all in good part and later let me buy him a treble whisky, on my expenses, on the night-train back to London, just to show there were no hard feelings.

After that came the hard slog which followed the Princess Margaret and Group Captain Townsend affair, and a fortnight in Paris trailing Princess Alexandra at her finishing-school and her weekly music lessons and her weekends at the home of the Comte de Paris and his eleven children, where the Princess caught the mumps and I spent miserable days knocking on the front door to ask how big her swellings were.

Then came the Geneva Conference and the first appearance of Krushchev and Bulganin, following the downfall of Malenkov, and it was about this time that I started to suffer from indigestion, from the worry of it all.

My instructions were to get inside the villas where the Big Four were having their important talks, but these places were so heavily guarded that even Anthony Eden's wife, Lady Eden, found herself locked out after going for a bathe in the lake and then returning with wet hair and a casual robe, and being unable to convince the guards that she was in fact the wife of the British Prime Minister.

Day after day, night after night, Mr Molotov refused to allow any journalists inside his villa. Then in the early hours of one night, not long before the dawn, the gates were suddenly, inexplicably, incredibly flung open. Only I wasn't there for this event, for which we had waited a week or more. I was fast asleep in my hotel bed, until I was woken by a kindly American journalist colleague on my bedside phone. It was not the first time that I realised that American reporters were different from Fleet Street ones. Magnanimous, disinterested, they could even afford to share a scoop, which was something we would rather die than do, as far as we in the British press were concerned. The journalist who married Margaret Truman (now Mrs Daniels) was like this. He used to read me his notes so that I could take them down carefully, verbatim!

I got back home, exhausted, to find myself down on the news schedule to fly to Russia. I didn't even have time to change my clothes, which explains why my modish straw picture hat with frontal velvet rosebud interest, which had been just right for the Hotel Beau Rivage in Geneva, took off in the high winds at Leningrad airport, leaving me standing pretty silly; but all those Tolstoyan figures with white beards to the waist and round-necked shirts dozing on the airfield suddenly came to life and gave chase. My hat, when I got it back only slightly air-swept, became, in those bleak days less than two years after the death of Stalin, the sensation of the Soviet Union.

CHAPTER XXV

BACK TO RUSSIA

I WAS THINKING OF all the Izvozchik boys and Grandma the day I got sent to Russia for the first time. I'd been waiting for a visa since the war ended, but it was not until Stalin died that the barriers were lifted. I had been with the Red Army on assignments in Mecklenburg; I'd danced with them at the Nuremberg trials —that is, at evening parties; but this was different. It felt like a sentimental journey. "Bednaya Olyechka" was going home at last. Going, thank God, with my British passport safely in my handbag.

The trouble with tourists who visited Russia was that they expected it to be terribly thrilling and mysterious and full of spies following them around. Some people became very annoyed when this didn't happen, and they kept turning round to look and there was no one following. It was insulting.

I was followed around a great deal, but only by people who were rather bored and wanted conversation. Apart from chess, conversation was still the main sport in the Soviet Union. They were very nearly as garrulous a people as the English, and much more interfering. Bossy, as well.

However, for me the pleasure was that nothing had changed. The air-crew who flew us from Helsinki were all unshaven and had beards like Grandpa's. Only two seats in the plane had safety-belts. The loud-speaker system broke down quite soon. I was travelling with Billy Wright and the Wolverhampton Wanderers en route for the football game versus Spartak, and a lot of the boys were sick because we flew so low, which made it rather rough.

At that time Moscow was hardly changed, except that the big ugly blocks of flats were just beginning to go up, so that in the dark it looked like Croydon. It is one of the hardships of journalism that you come close up to places you've only seen in books or dreams, and they look so different. Tokyo, for instance, did look so much like my home town of Birmingham, with all those little cycle shops, except, of course, that it was cleaner than Brum. But in the Moscow back streets—ah, that was different. The buildings, the narrow streets of little wooden houses warmed by kerosine stoves, the shops, the clothing were straight out of the 1880's, or even the 1860's. Girls with their heavy pigtails swept streets, old men in round-necked shirt-blouses dozed on benches. Life had not just been standing still; as though unable to move forward from the revolution, it had gone backwards into a sleepy past.

It was all I had hoped for, all I wanted. I wanted to shout, "Citizens, stop it!" when I came upon some workmen starting to demolish an old wooden house. It had a tiny chimney, no more than a little pipe in the roof, like the hovels round Grandma's house in the Kovno valley.

Everyone interfered with everyone else on the streets of Moscow.

"Citizeness, you can't cross there."

"Citizeness, it's no use waiting; the shop doesn't open until noon."

"I am only having a look in the window, citizen."

"But why, citizeness? There is only a stuffed fox there."

How could I tell him that is why I wanted to stare, fascinated? "They don't have such interesting dressmaking establishments in London," I said.

"You are . . . from *there*?" As though I had said "from the moon".

"Yes, citizen."

"Are you an English lady, then?"

"Not exactly. My grandparents were Russians."

"Tak." (so.)

The citizen lost interest immediately.

But other encounters lasted longer.

"Citizeness, where did you get those extraordinary shoes?"

My Italian sandals with wedge heels, embroidered with yellow raffia flowers, drew crowds everywhere.

"I bought them in Italy on holiday."

"Citizeness, you have been in Italy? How? When?"

A small crowd had gathered to listen. They examined me with close attention, from shoes to topknot of hair.

"But you are Soviet citizeness, so . . ."

"Not exactly."

"You speak in riddles, citizeness."

"She speaks with a strange foreign accent," said one of the crowd, now numbering perhaps twenty people.

"Polish, perhaps."

"Yes, I have a Polish niece who wears outlandish clothes," said someone.

"Her shoes are not outlandish."

"They are extravagant, then; flowers for the feet!"

"Now, then you idlers and chatterers, what's all the noise?"

The "militzia" (police) had arrived.

But it was not often that I was taken for a foreigner. For one thing, apart from looking like a Russian anyway, or, as Fleet Street colleagues always said, like "a refugee from the Kremlin", I soon discovered that I spoke Russian a lot better than many people sitting in the parks and gardens and strolling the scorching hot streets that summer. I met Poles and Latvians and Estonians and Lithuanians and even a blond Russian Jew standing, rather sadly, on the steps of the shabby synagogue in Spassoglinichevsky Street, who told me he was waiting for the "Schadchan", the marriage-broker. He waited all morning, but the man failed to turn up. So I told him about the girls in our lonely-hearts group at home, just longing for a husband. He became interested and animated. "How old are these girls?" He lapsed into gloom when I said, "a bit over thirty". He wanted a young girl, untouched, innocent, who could cook. He could get a Russian girl easily enough, but that was not what he wanted; they were rough, experienced. So then I told him about Grandma, and he said that was what he wanted.

It sounded strange. Then I remembered it was the first time in my life I'd ever heard anybody say anything nice about Grandma.

I never did go back to Utyena, though, not on any of my journeys into the Soviet Union. I never went back because I was told there was no one there. All the aunts had gone, and the cousins, and all their children, as well as mad Uncle Yasha and his children. The Nazis passed that way in 1941.

I went visiting old friends and relatives in Moscow, and in Leningrad too. But they were not all pleased to see me. For instance, going to see the woman friend of a cousin of mine living in the slums outside Moscow was a mistake.

The flat at the top of a broken-down building was clean enough, and the rooms were large. But it was too full of people; there seemed to be a family in every room, and my friend's room was no bigger than a box room, with only a bed and small table and chair.

My mistake was in going there boldly when the Stalin era had not yet ended. She was scared out of her wits to have a stranger from London just walking in out of the blue.

It was disconcerting, too, the way Russians told you the truth. In England we say "how are you?" and they say "Fine, thanks". It's always "fine", no matter what.

I said to my Russian friend, "Please don't let me put you out. I was in Moscow for the football, so I thought I'd just drop in and see how you were."

In answer I got a speech like the one Masha makes in *The Three Sisters*.

"My personal life has been a failure," she said. "I loved someone and he got tired of me. I tried to make friends with his children, but even that didn't work. So you see, I sit here and work." She was doing English translations. "I try to feel calm, but I feel I have failed in my life."

Well, what would you say? I think it would have sounded better if she had said it all in Russian. In English, which she spoke quite fluently, it sounded terrifying.

I ran away from that place; I thought how wise the English are. I must learn to be more English, I told myself.

Yet once, in Leningrad in 1960, I visited an elderly lawyer whom I knew only as Uncle Yasha. Yasha Fagin was Esther's uncle, her last surviving relative. It was like being in the poorer districts of Paris, like that street where my brothers-in-law Frenkel Frères had a factory in the rue Vieille-du-Temple. I mean, the block of flats in Leningrad had the same shabby, gracious look. Uncle Yasha's maid, Galina, opened the door. She had a big golden dog with her. They made a meal for me in his room. It was lovely. Nothing was changed. Even the furniture was exactly as it had been since before the revolution. There were huge dark mahogany sideboards, and everything was polished and gleaming. He said his life had been a success.

"I have had a happy life. I was in love with my wife until the end." He had the same directness. I had to hear it through. About his daughter who had married a prominent Communist. About the war and the siege of Leningrad. About each aunt and uncle who had lived and died. It was like listening to Father on the Izvozchiks, except that Uncle Yasha was full of love and praise for all of them. How different from Father!

So what was one to think of it all? I decided it must be really
tiring to live for any length of time in the Soviet Union. In
other countries people talk but do not say anything, which is often
a great relief. In Russia, I found, people talk all the time and they
are saying something each time, and it is exhausting; it is too
much.

CHAPTER XXVI

IN LOVE AGAIN

It is when you have stopped expecting happiness that it occurs.

I said nothing to anyone about it. Esther noticed that I had changed in some way, but I could not speak about it, even to her.

I was in love for the second and last time. We could never marry; quite a short story, therefore.

Physically, he was not the kind of man I had ever liked before. I admired thin, gaunt men with pale, hairless skin. J was huge and hairy, covered in it. He reminded me of that huge stuffed ape on the woman's bed in the Newcastle hotel room. He liked telling funny stories. I didn't like the stories much. We didn't agree on anything, not on politics or on much else. However, this man soon had such a hold over me that I felt I must have been tricked by some possibly sinister spell. Once, when he heard me giggling to myself, he said, "Now what is it?" He was rather sharp-tongued, and had no caressing manners of the kind I used to think were charming. I explained how Father always used to come home to us with presents, no matter how poor we were, sometimes second-hand books or partly-decaying oranges.

"Father used to put the presents on the table and say 'Here is something for Trilby. Now . . . you will see nothing, hear nothing, think of nothing but Svengali . . . Svengali'."

I said to J, still laughing:

"Now you are my Svengali."

"Perhaps," said J, "except that I shall not bring presents."

In my short married life all those years ago I had found kindness and tenderness, but not this time. Norbert used to say that he wanted to work hard and become rich so that he could give

me everything that a woman could want. I was surprised that
I had not realised earlier that this was one reason why he had died
so young. Some men who love their wives do, I think, worry
too much about giving them everything.

Love, in my opinion, should always be secret. If it is told to
others, shared with others, it is no longer your own, and through
this telling you may lose it in the end.

J and I spent a little time abroad discussing what we should do,
and decided to do nothing.

It was when we were in Brussels together that I began to find
out what he was really like.

We were sharing a flat, and were both rather hard up at the
time. I was rather proud of my cooking, but he did not greatly
admire it. He was used to something better. I wept because he
would not eat the carp which had taken me hours of labour to
prepare. He said, "You bore me when you are like this."

He got up and went out to a restaurant for a meal. I went to bed.
I was still sniffing slightly when he got home, though I tried not to
do so. I tried to control the sniffing, but tears ran down my nose
and started me off again.

He said he could not stand the sniffing. He went into the living-
room to sleep on the divan, taking most of the bedclothes with
him.

When we made it up next day, he tried to explain that what
had happened was my fault because I was over-eager and tried
too hard. In spite of earnestly wishing to understand, I could not
do so. When I asked him if perhaps I was the kind of woman who
had masochistic feelings, and this appealed to the sadist in him, he
replied that this was nonsense and that I analysed too much. He
said it was not altogether my fault, but those "damn Russians".
He said it was time I grew out of Russian habits and forgot about
the Russians.

"They are not nice people anyway," he said.

A telegram came from my editor telling me that I had to fly to Cyprus, where there was a lot of fighting going on. I was to spend two weeks in Cyprus, and after filing my story I should go on to Greece and the Lebanon and Jordan and do some feature stories.

So now I really had some reason for crying and sobbing. Our time together was strictly limited, and now we should be separated for weeks.

J said I was to stop crying and start preparing for the journey. He said it was good for me to have to work. The harder the work . . . and this was a difficult assignment . . . the better for me. He said: "Your trouble is that you are always too ready to be sorry for yourself; that is why I do not need to be at all sorry for you."

He said he was worried about his old father and felt sorry for him. "He has almost no money and does not get enough to eat. He is ailing, but he has to climb to the top of a tall building to his room. When I write and ask him how he is, my Father always says 'I am fine'. It is all right to feel sorry for people like that."

I said, "If I did not love you so much, I should hate you."

He said, "That makes sense to me."

We parted lovingly. I flew off from Brussels airport with a brave smile, but I could not help hoping that he would with his profound perception have seen the unshed tears behind it, and that he would admire my restraint. In the airport lounge I said jokingly, because I could not help myself, "You might say you like your new sporting comrade."

He laughed and said, "You are learning."

Before he finally left me, he found me a cottage in the country to live in. It was old, and had to have a lot of work done to it. Sometimes we would go and sit on a high hill near by where we could enjoy the view of the cottage and the hills beyond. But one day we arrived to find that there was a placard saying "For future development".

He said, "You mustn't grieve. Perhaps it will be a year before they start work, or even two years. You will have all that time to enjoy the view before it is spoiled."

Another time, sitting together at the opera, I suddenly thought that our own story was much more exciting, or so it seemed to me, than the love-story on the stage, even with Puccini added. Unlike the hero and heroine on that stage, we two were free humans with liberty to make a choice. To know that you have a choice about what you will do with your life is exhilarating.

The time raced by in those years, constantly threatened. But the sheer constancy of the threat, in the end, made me feel secure. How different from that young bride in her provincial security, complacent, timid.

Yet all this was a new handicap in my determination to exist and survive in a Fleet Street now itself facing decades of crises and upheavals. Even though it might be only in my mind, now I had a centre; I was anchored in the place where my happiness had been, and I did not want to leave it. But those were the years when the world was opening up after the war. I began to hate the aeroplanes that took me overseas to America, Russia, Rumania, the Middle East, the Far East. It seemed now a little absurd, this constant movement, this daily necessity of always going somewhere. I huddled down in seats on planes, trains, ships, and often wept foolishly, staring out ruefully into fields, clouds, white foam. What sort of hard-news reporter was I now? Where was the lust for adventure in this snivelling little woman? I even began, for the first time, to be afraid of flying. It was comic. I, the passionate suicide, was now afraid to die.

CHAPTER XXVII

I BECOME A STUNT GIRL

In 1956 I joined the *Daily Mail* and I was given my own column. I had arrived at last. Now people began to recognise me in the streets, because of the cartoons of Emmwood and Haro and Illingworth, showing the harassed, plump little woman, no longer young, with hairpins falling from her untidy topknot as she fled from job to job. The column was called "Frankly Yours", and the Greyhound Racing Association presented me with a greyhound by that name which I was to race at Harringay.

I was never madly keen on dogs or cold beer or outdoor sports which are played in winter. Now my life was filled with dogs and beer and football. Whole weeks I spent in hotels with the Russian teams Dynamo and Spartak. Then my evenings were spent compulsorily at the "dogs" or, worse still, behind scenes trying to cuddle my big black greyhound "Frankly Yours" for the photographer.

One thing led to another. My dog, a graceful eighteen-month-old animal of good birth, began to win. Prizes of nickel and chromium-plated beer jugs, ice buckets, candlesticks, cut-glass ashtrays littered my desk. People began to ring me up and ask how much they should bet on my dog, and became very annoyed when I said I frankly didn't know, chiefly because the mathematics of betting were quite beyond me. It all became a great worry, though in time I warmed slightly to my dog when I discovered that greyhounds did not, like so many other dogs, jump up upon you, which in my case would have been so inconvenient, as "Frankly Yours" was on the whole rather taller than me. I was photographed feeding her chocolate and patting her proud head in a gingerly way.

The upshot was that an invitation arrived for me to visit a Sheikh in the Lebanon, which at first made me feel that these desert chaps did perhaps have qualities to which Elinor Glyn and E. M. Hull, those writers of passionate desert love stories, had paid due tribute. I imagined, for example, that the Sheikh must have seen my photograph in the paper, and seen in it possibilities unnoticed by the less observant Englishmen. It was disillusioning therefore, a few weeks later, on being presented to Sheikh Allamuddin, head of the Druse tribe in Beirut, while staying at his expense in a hotel with swimming-pool entirely surrounded by bougainvillaea, to find that, although possessed of only one wife while being entitled to four, it was not in fact me at all whom he wanted to meet, but just my dog. "I've heard all about your dog and her great success at Harringay and elsewhere," said the Sheikh, beaming fondly at me, "so if you are willing to sell, I might decide to buy."

More than ever now I was known as the biggest "moaner" in the business. "What's the matter with you, then?" they'd say to me. "Off on a new lovely trip. Some people have all the luck." After all, it was all I'd dreamt of, wasn't it? There I was flying to Tokyo, to Hongkong, to Beirut and Israel. There I was walking up the long, steep hill to Bethlehem, the usual quarrelsome and resentful photographer at my back. I was swimming off Cyprus, or flirting with the army or the air force in their comfortable clubs. I was gossiping with the Onassis family on their yacht in Piraeus harbour at Athens, sleeping in the late King Carol's old love-nest at Sinaia near Bucarest, dining on the Magareten island at Budapest to the music of the little Hungarian band, gnawing chicken bones Henry VIII style at Grinzing near Vienna, I was back again in Moscow, Leningrad, Berlin, Stockholm. I began to wear a sort of sulky, more or less permanently aggrieved expression.

The trouble was—and I knew it—that I was stricken with the common Fleet Street disease. Having fought and trained and struggled, as we all had to in those years, to become a top by-lined newspaper reporter in the famous Street itself, we were soon fighting and struggling to get out of it. Partly this happened to us because we all went mad quite quickly. Even the sanest, most charming people have gone down under the strain of it.

"Why is that girl crying?" said William Hardcastle, then our deputy editor. I couldn't even let my beloved friend know that I would not be there when he came, after a long, long absence and many difficulties, by air and sea to visit me. Because, long before he could arrive, I should be on a slow boat from Copenhagen to Leningrad, to follow poor Nina Ponomareva (that Nina who had fancied five silly hats in C & A Modes) home to Russia.

"Why burst into hysterical screams," said my features editor, Marius Pope (who later became features boss on the *Evening Standard*), "when I'm so nice to you that I give you a superb wine-tasting tour for a fortnight, just doing nothing but soaking the wine and the sun up and down the coast of Spain and Portugal?"

But these were only minor reasons why we all, having reached the Street, dreamed of escaping from it.

I think the real reason was that we all became quickly vain about having our names, in big, in the paper nearly every day. Quite soon it was no novelty; in fact, it wasn't good enough. I knew several men who used to carry their fan letters about the office, showing them to anyone who would stop and listen. Only people in newspaper offices never did stop and listen, if they could help it.

Those fan letters. In our saner moments we all knew that many came from quite lonely people longing to establish contact with others.

Those fan letters, which said we ought not to be on a paper used for wrapping fish and chips or making firelighters. We ought to be in hard covers. We were literature. Boy, that's what it says! Right here. Look at this letter from Mrs . . . .! Just read what she says about my piece from Kyle of Lochalsh. Go on, man *read* it!

Is a newspaper really a nut-house, then? What, all of them? Well, no, not really. . . . But when the whole thing stopped, that was the time when you found out. And already it was stopping. For many of us. It was coming to an end.

Those fan letters were being sent elsewhere. To those charming news announcers, with the nice smiles and wavy hair, on television.

Meanwhile I was getting fat, and it was this that made my name.

A friend of mine named Larry Solon, who used to be editor of *Woman*, once said to me, "When I heard you'd got into Fleet Street, then I was very sad because I knew your story couldn't have a happy ending."

Larry was right, of course. Except that in fact I was a happy little woman nearly all the time now. And there's nothing in the world so fattening.

One of the hardships of life, I have always found, is that people were always too keen to be sorry for one. I never could understand it. And a lot of people in our business became very sorry for me because the paper was turning me into a sort of funny girl. Some people thought clowning was not a woman's job. They thought it unsexing, for one thing. This was a limited view, though, of human experience. It was well known that male clowns were sad in private but female ones were even more varied. Mae West, when I met her, was businesslike and rather refined; the clowning was strictly for business only. Sophie Tucker, whenever I talked to her in private, was inclined to gloom, and a hacking cough. And Dame Margaret Rutherford was, I found, in real life rather swooning, romantic, sexy-sensitive with a handsome and devoted husband to match.

People were, in fact, almost never what they seemed, and it proved to be one of the blessings of journalism that gave you the chance to see and to know this. I could see now why Father himself had always wanted to be a journalist and reporter. His favourite story, which he called Miss Shum's Husband (but which was actually one of Conan Doyle's), and which he loved telling, was about the miserable beggar who was really a rich, bourgeois husband. I saw why he loved telling us about Abie, his big brother, who was the Good Son and kept a mistress and three children. Or about Phoebe, the capable business woman who was always putting her foot in it. I suppose it did help me, though, to succeed in this clowning business, while it lasted, that I didn't ever feel I was myself at all. I was really being Father all the time.

I thought when I got up to eleven stone that it was the end of my career in Fleet Street. I told Beryl about this. She was furious at my being fat, but in her letter she enclosed an extract she had typed out from a book by Walter Duranty, the American journalist who wrote *I write as I please*. Mr Duranty thought his career as a reporter was over too when he lost a leg in a train accident and had to get a wooden one. Until he found he could turn this handicap into an asset. He was no longer just journalist Duranty, but the reporter with the wooden leg, and it made him.

But how could this help me? A big bottom, I felt, got a girl nowhere, except to leave her sitting about on it. At least this made a change after all those tiresome flights abroad, eating too much smoked salmon, caviar with champagne.

I brooded on the problem. One day the features editor shouted across the room. "You're wanted." It was the start of the diet era. Diets, said the editor, were jolly good for circulation, especially with a daily diet sheet given away free, so to speak, with each copy of the paper. I had to hand over all my remaining chocolate peppermints and the packet of buttered walnuts I kept in my drawer. The story of my privations, with shrinking cartoons of me by Emmwood, ran for several weeks. Then I had to do it all over again, this time with exercises too, and new, much more flattering cartoons, this time by Illingworth.

When it was over I was not noticeably thinner, but I was now launched upon a new career. I was to be a sort of jolly clown woman with whom the overweight British woman could identify. And to demonstrate, I had to do a series of stunts. I believe I was the first Stunt Girl on the *Daily Mail*.

First I was squeezed into a 38″ pale blue, much-stretched skirt of regulation Pan-American air hostess uniform, and sent to be an apprentice air hostess on the Luxury President Special to New York and back. Nobody mentioned that a girl swelled at 30,000 feet, which was why air-stewardesses in those planes usually changed into slippers, only I swelled all over. Father would have loved it, the way the zip on that 38″ skirt flew off me and hit the nearest champagne bottle, to the surprise of the luxury passengers.

Then I was bus clippie for a day on a No. 14 bus in the much more flattering navy serge uniform provided by London Transport.

It began to catch on. Everyone tried to think of new stunts for me to do. I was a waitress, teacher, hospital nurse on night duty at East Dulwich hospital, policewoman, private detective, lost-property attendant at Waterloo station, washing machine demonstrator, deck-chair attendant on Margate beach, all-night lorry-driver's all-night mate, sewing-lady in a royal couture house, pop-singer, film-actress, saxophone-player (I nearly swallowed the instrument) with Ivy Benson's all-girl band, usherette, window-dresser for Dickins & Jones, glove salesgirl for Selfridges, and so on. In between I pursued Princess Grace of Monaco, visited ex-King Zog of Albania, dug a hole in the road on the M1 highway, took part in jet-flight stunts to Cannes and Moscow and Cyprus and Greece. Now and then I had hysterics. During these my boss shouted, "Get that damn woman out of here", and he locked himself in the lavatory until it was safe to come out.

But the trouble with a newspaper was that, like a marriage, it had to keep going day after day. In the end there were no stunts left.

"There must be something," said the features editor. "Couldn't you go and be a Liberal Party candidate or something, or do a turn in a circus?"

They toyed with the idea of sending me up in a balloon over the Alps, and I was all set, reluctantly, to go, when luckily the wind changed.

The end came when he sent me to try and be Peter Pan and fly across the stage in a new Christmas production. The producer said there was a special harness for this, but none to fit me.

The F.E. was not pleased. "You've fallen down again," he said as he helped himself to the tray of codeine and other tranquillisers which his secretary prepared with his morning tea.

I was saved, for the time being, by the discovery of a so-called "wonder-drug" in an old people's clinic in Bucarest, Rumania. I was sent for a fortnight or so to stay with the old people. "And mind you have all the injections and treatments. We're not trying anything out on our customers unless it's been tried on you first."

CHAPTER XXVIII

I DISCOVER THE RUMANIAN YOUTH
DRUG H3

ACTUALLY IT WAS Esther who discovered H3. She'd found a
new dentist in Kensington and was always singing his praises. So
kind, so gentle he was. He was a young German who took refuge
in Bucarest during the war, and had qualified there as a dental
surgeon.

One Saturday afternoon Esther arrived for our visit together
to a theatre matinée. She had aged considerably since she had
stopped giving Russian lessons, and was now extremely frail. We
liked the matinées, as it was easier to get seats in the cheaper parts
of the theatre, and she did not have to go home in the dark
through the immensely long streets behind Olympia. Esther,
who had fled from her home in Russia and then had to flee again
from Vienna, was nervous of the large number of Indian and
African neighbours who now lived all round her. She had what
amounted to a passion for the theatre, and during the intervals,
we discussed each play in Russian, thinking ourselves incompre-
hensible to other theatre-goers. More often than not, however,
some lonely Russian or Pole—once it was a young Persian girl
and once it was a Frenchwoman—would follow us to a coffee-
house and attach herself to us until we had to shake her off.

On this Saturday Esther arrived in great excitement. Her
Rumanian dentist had told her of a remarkable Youth Drug
which had recently been discovered in Rumania. The curtain
was about to go up at St Martin's that day before we could get
to the point of it. Esther had the Russian taste for putting in all
the details. Nothing must be left out. There must be nothing

"superficial" in her version of this Rumanian "miracle".

"He was doing some fillings. And who knows how long it will be that I can keep these last few teeth. 'Starost, nye radost', I said to him. Ach, there is no pleasure in getting old. And he took a letter out of his pocket and it was from his seventy-five-year-old uncle in Bucarest. Now I know you will laugh, but I became very excited when I realised that this could be a good story for you for your paper. His uncle wrote to say that he had gone to a clinic for treatment for gangrene of the leg, and that a month or so later he came out cured. No, no, be quiet, that is not the point of the story. The uncle wrote, 'Now I am springing about like a youngster and my grey hairs are turning black'. The uncle said he had been given injections of a wonder-drug called H3 by the head of the clinic, whose name was Professor Ana Aslan, and that all the patients in the clinic said they felt they were getting younger because their white hairs went black at the roots and their wrinkles started to disappear."

It certainly sounded like a scoop to me. Next day, on my usual Sunday duty, I tried our library in Northcliffe House to see if there were any cuttings about a woman doctor named Aslan. I found a little piece, about three paragraphs, reporting a recent international Medical Congress of doctors held in Italy, where a Rumanian woman doctor had spoken of her experiments with a remarkable rejuvenating drug which she called H3. That was all. I reported this to my features editor, Marius Pope, who became excited about it. "You must go to Rumania immediately," he said, "and find out the truth. If it turns out to be a phoney story, then we will say so. But if it is true, boy, what a story."

He hoped, he said, for both our sakes that the story was true. "Then I get not only a super scoop," he said, "but a new, lithe, youthful Olga skimming about the office. Hooray."

He told me first of all to ring Professor Aslan and ask her to try and expedite a visa for me from her end.

This was October 1958. It took me until January to get a visa. At that time, only two years after the Hungarian uprising, few British journalists were able to get visas for Rumania or Hungary.

The only western transport, then, was by the Belgian airline Sabena, which flew three times a week from Brussels via Cologne and Budapest. The plane landed, rather unsteadily, on an airport rocky with built-up ice and snow. Bucarest in January was fiercely cold.

I was given a suite at the Atheneé Palace Hotel close by the former royal palace, and just before midnight Professor Aslan telephoned to welcome me.

Next morning at 8.30 I was taken by car for the short drive to the clinic. There was no traffic; a few people clambered on to the trams or picked their way carefully over the pavements, rocky and dangerous with hillocks of hard ice.

Through the pretty driveway we went up to a gracious white three-storey building. The heat hit my face as I entered the porch and made it hard to climb the two flights of stairs, while wearing a wool-lined overcoat.

So many people have praised me, so many have blamed me, for launching the drug H3 upon the world that I must tell this story, step by step, exactly as it happened, and leave the reader to judge the truth for himself. Any reporter, I feel, would have done as I did—and many followed me later to do the same—and that was to report factually what I had seen and heard. I had no knowledge of medicine then, and I had none later.

Certainly there were many features about the clinic which were unusual, and which I recognised as such because our Mother had been a qualified hospital nurse and so was my youngest sister Bettina, who was a gold-medallist SRN and midwife, so that I knew how doctors and nurses normally behave in a hospital or clinic. Still, this was not England but Rumania, and this was a Latin people resembling in most things the Italians, and therefore I assumed that this might explain why, for example, a journalist like myself was allowed to wander freely from room to room, from laboratory to out-patients, to examine all the case-histories and photographs, and was shown—and this seemed the oddest of all—the messages, telegrams, letters of recommendation amounting to ecstasy from doctors, nurses and patients from all over the world.

Professor Aslan was a charmer, then about sixty-four years of age. She came of a cultivated family. Her manner to me was warm and affectionate to a degree that no English doctor would have permitted herself to show to a journalist in similar circumstances. She protested that she wanted no publicity at the same time that she gave me all the facilities I could possibly wish for . . . and even in remote Rumania (as it was at that time) they had heard of the *Daily Mail*, and knew what a report appearin the paper could mean to the clinic.

It was therefore bewildering, and yet I was able to find an explanation for the unusual things happening all round me. The Professor clearly wanted recognition from western doctors, because this alone could set the seal on her achievement.

Her story was disarming in its modesty and concern for her sick and elderly patients. She made no claim to have discovered anything new. She claimed only that, by rediscovering a remedy discovered in the twenties by a German doctor and later discarded, she had by accident stumbled on a treatment which resulted in a general "Verjungung" of the body, meaning a kind of "rejuvenation".

Professor Aslan, formerly a heart specialist in private practice, had been put in charge of a large Rumanian hospital. One day it was noticed that a patient who had been treated with injections of procain showed not only a remarkable improvement in his condition but also signs of returning youth. Professor Aslan decided to make large-scale experiments, and injections of procain were given, sub-cutaneously or sometimes intramuscularly, to senile or elderly patients in the geriatric wards. At the same time laboratories were set up to test the drug on hundreds of rats and mice. The results were so encouraging that the Professor was put at the head of this clinic in Bucarest, where the treatment had been carried out over a period of ten years.

Day after day for a fortnight I visited the clinic and interviewed patients, especially those who were Russian-speaking, as many were. Many patients had come from the Soviet Union and from all over the Balkans, so that it was a relief to switch from my awkward German and French to talk freely with patients in Russian.

I was shown bald men and women whose hair was regrowing, or had fully grown again; there were patients who told me of their recovery from stroke, thrombosis, encephalitis, arthritis, and so on. But the main feature of all these alleged "cures" was the change brought about in their health and appearance by a long treatment of procain injections given three times a week, with short rests, over a long period of months or even years. I went from bed to bed and room to room where gay, chatty men of ninety years and 100 and 102, and even older, asked me to examine the roots of their white heads. Even among the elderly I could see, particularly at the back of the neck, the regrowth of black hairs among the white. A woman patient undressed to show me how shapely her breasts had become; a woman opera singer of over eighty who had not sung for years sang arias for me. And the aged patients in their dressing-gowns gathered at the door to listen.

It was the oddest clinic. Every few minutes, during my long talks with Professor Ana Aslan and her deputy Dr Cornel David and others, patients would suddenly burst into the room with a casual "Scusi" because they wanted a little chat with the Professor. One Russian woman was impatient because the brown hair was returning only in patches upon her bald head (the condition known as alopecia), and wanted reassurance that she would have a fine head of hair in the end.

In the afternoons I too was given an injection. ("We're not giving it to our readers until it's been tried out on you," the editor had said.) Then Professor Aslan would have her own injection or supervise the same treatment for her nurses and assistants. A short course of procain gave her energy, she said. She worked from 6 a.m. daily until midnight and later, and at sixty-four she was a glowing, rounded and attractive woman.

How did it work? Alas, here was the snag. She didn't know, she said it frankly. She could only guess that the procain stimulated ageing cells; she felt also that it acted on the body as a vitamin does. Meanwhile, she longed for Britain to show an interest in her work.

The Rumanian Government of the People's Republic had set up a factory for manufacturing the drug H3. She had perfected her own formula containing vitamins and stabiliser, as one of the snags of the treatment was that procain quickly lost its potency, and therefore it was important to know the exact ingredients of the Rumanian injection.

The *Daily Mail* ran the story in a series of five articles in February 1959. It was called the Youth Drug, and I think the whole thing aged me as nothing else did, chiefly because, once started, it seemed impossible to stop. Letters arrived in sacks, with telegrams and phone calls from all over the world, especially from Japan and India, where men are always keen to stay young as long as possible.

Worst of all were the people who called to see me. They came from Sydney, Australia, Mexico and Brazil. They told the commissionaire in the hall they they had spent their life savings on making the journey. A group of Indian gentlemen said they would just sit there quietly in the hall under our photograph of Lord Northcliffe and wait for me to come downstairs, even if it took six months.

I was followed in the streets and on buses by strange men from Dublin who said they were doctors, and several millionaires and one duke got their solicitors to ring me up to make a dinner date to discuss the whole thing. Paul Getty and I became friendly over the whole matter, although Mr Getty said there might after all be nothing in the drug really, but it was nice that someone was still working on the problem of wonder drugs to make old people young.

Meanwhile the deluge of letters continued throughout the summer, and now and then I had hysterics and stayed at home in bed, saying I could no longer cope.

The trouble was that at that time Rumania was still totally under Communist influence and there was no communication with the west. It was no use my sending out thousands of circular letters giving Aslan's telephone number or address at the Institutul de Geriatrie, Strada Monastirea Caldarusani 9, Bucarest. I had seen her study piled with letters in all languages, but correspondence was painfully slow and there was a censorship on all of them. More than three hundred of the thousands of letters I had received were from doctors asking for more information.

At last the editor (Arthur Wareham) decided that we should invite Professor Aslan to come to London at our expense, to address meetings of those doctors interested.

Meanwhile, an English doctor named Richard Mackarness had taken the matter up on our behalf. He wrote an article in the paper giving support to H3 from a medical point of view. He named other doctors who had made similar experiments, including those by Dr Raymond Greene, brother of Graham Greene, who had published his findings on the use of procain in the treatment of rheumatoid arthritis, at the Royal Society of

Medicine, London, in 1949. But later I heard that Dr Greene, like the others, had discarded the treatment.

Why had it been dropped? Dr Mackarness's explanation was that cortisone had been discovered at that point, and this had shown more dramatic results. Also the treatment with procain (it is known as novocain in East Germany, from where the drug comes, and is used by dentists as an anaesthetic) was long and slow and inconvenient, requiring constant injections and supervision. Only Dr Aslan had used it over a long period on thousands of people.

For my part, it was a relief to know that help was on the way. I could easily be recognised, because of Emmwood's cartoons, and for months I dreaded calling a taxi or taking a bus. There were also the men-of-uncertain-age who kept ringing to invite me to dinner, pretending they'd developed a passion for me, though they could hardly wait to finish the soup course before they started on about H3 and could I get it for them?

That summer Dr Mackarness and I were sent to Germany, Austria and Switzerland to check on all the "Verjungung" treatments and to talk to continental doctors using the Aslan methods or similar.

We got back to a new flood of letters and visits and cables. The H3 story had by now been re-told in local papers throughout North and South America and the United States. Determined American ladies started to arrive from California and sat in our hall, waiting for me to appear.

In November 1959 Professor Aslan arrived, looking years younger and declaring that it was not only H3 which was responsible, but the happiness of coming to England to meet "the wonderful English doctors". We took her to a hotel in Kensington, from which from time to time she was "kidnapped" by doctors and others claiming, in the strangest French, to be from Egypt or Saudi Arabia or Montevideo and even from Monaco.

Barbara Cartland (Mrs Hugh McCorquodale) gave a party for Aslan, and members of the Government came. She was taken to the House of Lords and to the opera, and to visit geriatric clinics in Leeds and London. She complained that the British senile looked half dead already, and I knew what she meant. They had certainly been a jolly, even ribald lot of patients in her clinic in Bucarest. (This, however, was one of the things which helped to spoil her case later on with British doctors, who declared, that if you make old people very cosy and happy, then obviously they will look younger and get younger, without any of the drug H3.) But in the first week the Professor was radiant, talking all the time in a torrent of French, in which she was due to give her lectures at the Apothecaries Hall, Blackfriars, and which would be simultaneously translated by a French-Canadian doctor, Dr S. Duckett.

Alas, her visit was a failure in the end. Doctors declared themselves dissatisfied with her lectures. The final damning conclusion was given in a strong article in the *British Medical Journal* on 27 November 1959, which paid tribute to Aslan's charm and to her "vast therapeutic optimism". But her work with H3 was attacked. She had failed to meet scientific requirements, which demanded that "blind, controlled tests" must be made according to British and American medical practice before any claims could be made. This meant giving the drug to a controlled group, which must be matched in every way, and must include those getting not the drug itself, but just plain water.

Professor Aslan said she did not make these tests, partly for humane reasons, and partly because such tests, if they were to be truly effective and conclusive, required a vast sum of money, an entire residential clinic, teams of doctors, nurses and statisticians. Rumania was too poor for it, and, besides, she felt that her controlled tests on animals were sufficient, together with all the other evidence she had collected. Make your own tests, she said, and give a decision about H3. But it was too late. Rival newspapers rushed in to publicise the stronger parts of the *B.M.J.* report and H3 was, for the time being, discredited.

I said goodbye to Ana Aslan at London Airport. Her face was sad. She held a copy of the *British Medical Journal* to her breast. This was the copy containing the article which said that H3 was not, and could not be, the benefactor to mankind that the Rumanian woman doctor claimed it was. Admittedly, the writer said, it was well known that repeated injections of procain do quite often tend to improve hair and skin conditions, even causing re-pigmentation in some cases. But this could not, thundered the *B.M.J.*, be called "a rejuvenation".

Professor Aslan said, "British doctors have condemned H3 without even trying it themselves, and without attempting to make the controlled tests which they claim could provide the proof of its therapeutic value."

So we parted . . . and I thought, well, that's the end of the story. Only it was not.

CHAPTER XXIX

THE SEQUEL—TO THE H3 STORY

I SOON FOUND THAT the attack by the *British Medical Journal* (representing a large section of British doctors) did not result, as I had hoped, in stopping the flow of letters, phone calls and visits. There were doctors who still wanted to try it out for themselves; there were doctors who felt there had been some reservations in the British medical "mind" because H3 had come from a Communist-dominated country. Others felt there might have been discrimination against a woman—particularly as all agreed that Aslan was rather charming—while on the other hand others tended to think it was ridiculous that a little country like Rumania, without a tradition of scientific research and with nothing to boast about, bar some rather romantic ex-kings and a lot of oil wells and not enough educated technicians to run them properly, should produce a treatment which, if it did nothing else, could postpone old-age. Thousands of patients wrote to say that they believed British doctors were too conservative anyway, and would I please supply them with phials of H3 and the name of a doctor who would prescribe and give the treatment. I sent out thousands of circulars telling them to *read* the *British Medical Journal* of 27 November 1959 and to trust their own doctor.

It was no use. I felt desperate. Even ex-Queen Helen of Rumania was sorry for me, though when she granted me an interview I soon realised that it was because she wanted some news . . . any news . . . of her home, her servants and staff. She was, literally, the only person who never asked me for supplies of H3—and when I saw her rather beautiful face and figure I could see the reason why she had no interest in it.

Things continued like this for another year.

Meanwhile British geriatric societies in Britain arranged for some tests to be made, and the results were negative. Aslan was angry. She wrote me to say that a mere three-month test with a tiny "control" group of patients was worse than useless, as some patients showed no improvement until the end of a six- or twelve-month treatment. Above all, England had not obtained supplies of her own Rumanian formula but had used ordinary procain available from British Drug Houses.

By this time many patients had managed to obtain a visa, and had gone to Rumania to try and get treatment at the clinic. A new wing was opened to accommodate foreign out-patients, and a firm of agents established themselves in London to handle supplies. Invitations for Aslan arrived from all over, and for the next two or three years she spent six months of the year going round the world, lecturing and talking to doctors. She stayed with President Nkrumah and his family (then at the height of his popularity) and then with ex-President Soekarno. She toured Egypt and Mexico and Vietnam and visited America. The late "Red Dean", the Rev. Hewlett Johnson, who had been one of her earliest patients, declared that the health of the Chinese leaders depended on their regular supplies of H3.

I was asked to write a book about Aslan, and she and I spent a week together in Copenhagen so that I could get the latest information. On this occasion all her former sadness had gone. She showed me some of her presents, from Nkrumah and Soekarno and many, many more.

Her deputy Dr Cornel David was with her, and they told me the secret of their present excitement and optimism.

A group of doctors in Chicago, attached to a medical college there (not the university) were interested in H3. For nearly a year they had been testing it—this time using her own formula, which she herself supplied—on a number of controlled groups of elderly and senile patients in geriatric homes in and around Chicago. These were the blind, controlled tests demanded. Some groups were being injected with nothing but plain water, others with H3, and proper statistical analyses were to be published shortly. "I have spoken with the leading doctor by telephone," Aslan told me, "and he says the results are encouraging."

The following year the results were announced at a medical conference in Boston. Some eight Chicago doctors stated that the results of their tests with H3 were sufficiently encouraging to justify further investigations being made. On 1 January 1964, the *New York Times* published an account of the Chicago investigations and an interview with one of the doctors. The paper said the whole matter of the drug H3 had been too hastily dropped and, in the light of the Chicago report, it should be reopened.

But it was too late. The impetus had gone. No one came forward to undertake the work, and there—somewhat to my relief, I do admit—the matter rested.

I leave the last word, gladly, to our own Dr Alex Comfort, scientist and specialist in gerontology (the study of old age). In his recent book *The Process of Ageing* he wrote:

"The world and public reaction to the claims made by Rumanian workers for procain as a palliative of age changes was an object lesson in how not to assess an over-confident clinical claim. It had long been known that this local anaesthetic had some effects, in big doses, which appeared worth investigating; it has, for example, marked effects on heat-regulation.

"Over-enthusiastic claims from Rumania that it reversed age changes were the signal for some acrimonious politico-medical rows at conferences, and one of the most depressing spates of bad work, both pro and contra, in recent medical history.

"At the end of it all we still do not know whether procain has any useful effects on the ills of age, its discoverer's claims being uncritically optimistic, and the refutations being based on rush series done on handfuls of patients. Procain is at least generally admitted to be quite harmless, which is more than can be said of some other remedies. But we would still like to know whether it does anything, if so what it does, and whether any observed effects are due to the drug or to suggestion. The atmosphere of 'needle' surrounding this study, as so often in the past where age has been involved, has not really been conducive to finding out."

CHAPTER XXX

BACK TO RUSSIA AGAIN

So, WITH ONE thing and another, it was tough going between 1959 and 1960.

There was the rough stuff at the start of the Krushchev tour to meet President Eisenhower at Camp David, in that terrible Indian summer of '59, when I was sent to follow Madame Krushcheva across the U.S.A.

We moved in the wake of the Krushchev family—Nikita and Nina and the three children, Julia (Nina's stepdaughter, in her late thirties) and Nina's own children, Rada and Sergey—we were like some vast army in solid massed formation, several thousand strong.

It was not just that we represented the papers, cinemas, magazines, television companies, journals and weeklies of every nation and race in the world, but we even had the representatives of papers which did not exist, from corners of the world that no one had ever heard of. It was, after all, the first visit of a Russian leader to America.

We had simply everybody in our party, even one pretty woman in a rather advanced stage of pregnancy, the late Marguerite Higgins from the *New York Herald Tribune*. She was the coolest and most intrepid of all of us, and when the Russian party —big enough to occupy a whole half a railway train or a whole jet plane to themselves—saw Marguerite coming in her navy silk dress, holding her head slightly backwards as pregnant women do, the Russians, bred to show a proper respect for motherhood, parted like the Red Sea and let her through. The result was that she got more scoops than any of the sweating hundreds of us, champing away on the fringes of this vast army.

Unwashed, unkempt and mostly unshaven because there wasn't time, with our bundles of dirty washing stacked under the seats, American army planes rather slower than the big jet carrying Mr K. whirled us night by night, sleepless and smelling soon quite evilly of spilled whisky sour, of smoke and sweat, from New York to Washington and San Francisco to Hollywood, Des Moines in Iowa, Pittsburgh, and back to Washington.

At the start there was the famous railway journey from Washington to San Francisco, which was our very first chance of getting, if we could, an exclusive scoop from the K family. The French made up the largest and most efficient and elegant party. Even unwashed, they somehow smelled better than we did. They were a most superior crowd, including many from *Paris Match*, and sometimes made a point of having hysterics at the sight of real American cooking. One beautiful dark girl from *Elle* magazine always took one look at the chicken Maryland or the blueberry pies and shrieked to the waiters or waitresses, "Tekk away . . . 'orreeble . . . eet ees 'orreeeeble!" It made, naturally, a great impression on all of us.

We collapsed on to the train, dazed by the heat, half-dozing over the griddle cakes with maple syrup served in the breakfast car, when suddenly the loud-speaker started to crackle.

"Ladies and Gentlemen of the Press," said a voice that clearly came from the head of American police and detectives who made up a whole separate army moving among us, "your ATTENTION please. Chairman Krushchev is coming through the train. Do not panic, any of you. Stay where you are. Keep your seats *please*. The Chairman is coming right through the train and will speak with each one of you."

Chaos followed. Cameramen tried to rush back to their own compartments to collect their equipment; some went fore and some went aft; there was the crunch of shattered glass as those already with their equipment fought to save it from the mêlée, but in vain. Right through the corridor of the train, stretching from the engine back to the rear half belonging to the Russian party and guarded by American police, a solid mass of flailing, struggling, sweating bodies fought to move in one direction or another. Some, less certain of the English language anyway, were not quite sure what was happening and thought the train must be on fire. Arabs, Indians, Greeks, every nation on earth joined in the fight. Trapped photographers swarmed over people's heads and shoulders and climbed into the luggage racks, either to get a new angle or to save their cameras from destruction.

I was usually quite good in a panic—souvenir, perhaps, from war-time days and nights of bombing in Fleet Street. Getting down on my hands and knees—I had already done this on the first day for the arrival at Washington airport, and it had worked supremely well—I worked my way steadily through the mass of squirming legs and feet, and at last penetrated through the blocked corridor until I reached the Russian half of the train. And there he was, Nikita himself, a radiant little figure in silver grey, ready for his triumphal tour, I grabbed hold of his arm, and after that I never let go.

I think Mr K was the only one who enjoyed that ride. He loved, clearly, being squeezed and pummelled and held: it made him feel good; it made him feel popular. Until he got to the end of the train. There, in the last compartment, was a bar, a little blessed space, and crouched over her typewriter sat *Elle*, a striking figure in black cloak.

Mr K stopped, and looked, and made a sign. His interpreter bent down graciously and said, "Chairman Krushchev would like to meet you."

She looked up for a moment, then calmly resumed her typing. "Jane!" I gasped. Perhaps she had not understood.

"Why should I spikk with 'im?" said Jane to me. "I do not

want to meet 'orreeeble man, An' 'is wife, she 'ave orreeeble legs."

As I said, the French were a cut above us all, really. And anyway, *Elle* had only sent her along to write about the "fashions".

Later in New York, huge crowds gathered. The charming Nina queened it at the Waldorf Astoria, in her hair-net, admired by all for her poise and simplicity.

Outside, struggling with the sweating crowd, were two middle-aged New York cops, shouting in Russian, trying, apparently, to pacify and control the crowds. The older one's father had come from Utyena too; only "Poppa" had gone on to Liverpool instead of landing at Grimsby.

Between assignments I got offers, as we all did, to go on free trips for the inaugural flight of a new airline. Then came the first BEA Comet flights to Moscow in April 1960, when I was invited by that favourite of mine, and favourite of most of us, Squadron-Leader Bill Simpson, author of an autobiography *I burned my fingers*. "Come on a jolly," he would phone to say. He always called these trips "jollies". On one plane to Moscow went writers like Graham Greene, and on the other went reporters like me.

Emmwood (real name—John Wood) reluctantly came with me. He liked gardening and the golf club, and he didn't like Russians or flying. He looked down as we flew into Moscow airport. There had been daffodils in his Kentish garden; here there was just snow. "I must have been mad to listen to you," said Emmwood. There'd be wolves, too, most likely in those woods round Moscow.

A large, heated car rushed us through the forests of Christmas trees on the high road from Vnukovo airport.

"Are there wolves?" I asked the driver.

"Nichevo" he said. "Never mind, only a few."

We neared the new skyscraper flats of the city. They seemed unending and ugly, like those in Birmingham and London.

Our hotel, the Ukraine, had a huge Gothic spire on top, like a church. On the eighth floor we had suites of big rooms with imitation parquet, private bathrooms, radio sets, telephones. Double suites had TV also. Flower prints were on the walls. This was the new, modern, thawing Russia I hadn't seen for five years. Emmwood said it all looked like Euston Station without the trains.

One day we went to see Moscow's *Punch*, a magazine of cartoons and caricatures called *Krokodil*. At first we couldn't find No. 28, Yamskaya Polya, and Emmwood wanted to give up and do some drawing. "Let's drop it," he said. Even if Mr Malcolm Muggeridge did say it was all right with his letter of introduction, we might get brain-washed.

When we found the place, the editor, Mr Wilensky, and all the *Krokodil* cartoonists were pleased to see us. They put us on a divan and Mr Yuriev brought wine and oranges. Emmwood kept giving me meaningful looks. Now for the brain-wash.

Instead, when we'd sucked all the oranges, they brought pencils and paper and put us both to work.

"You'll be paid," said Mr Wilensky firmly. "In roubles too."

Well, we were a bit short of those. And our food coupons from Intourists were all eaten too. Emmwood whispered to me, "Better get on with it, then."

He did some drawings and I did the captions. "If the golf club could see me now," said Emmwood.

It was over two hours later when they released us.

"Well, we belong to the workers now," said Emmwood, as they saw us down the steps all slippery with ice and snow. Mr Wilensky and Mr Yuriev said they felt a bit worn out, having to start work at 11 a.m. every day, and they couldn't always think what to put in the paper. And then we'd turned up in the nick of time.

Anyway, I said, as we went back to the hotel, we can always blame it all on Mr Muggeridge if anything goes wrong.

After that we went to the Ippodrom for the trotting races. We paid four roubles each and went inside the posher part; it was just like Harringay, only freezing cold, with men streaming in from the Metro (the tube-station) nearby. They wore flat caps or tall fur hats, and they strode past us very fast to make their "pari", their bets.

I'd warned Emmwood about his rather fancy tweed hat, and in between the races it started to attract a lot of attention.

So we went to buy a programme to study the form. "How do your choose your horse?" we asked one of the crowd of men who kept following, to stare at us, or rather to stare at Emmwood's hat. He said he just had a good look at the horses beforehand, and he knew pretty well what each could do, as he was a regular. You placed a bet either for first or second place, but if you picked a favourite your winnings wouldn't be much, of course.

We went downstairs to the betting booths. These were in a large, glamorous, heated hall where caviar and other food and soft drinks were on sale. It looked as though it had been a former palace of the Czars, with fine decor in pale green and marble. We placed bets of five roubles each and went back to the stands, but soon there was a crowd round us again. They'd spotted Emmwood's striped shirt and elegant navy jacket. "Look, John," I said, "shall we write off the ten roubles and get away while you've still got your shirt and jacket on?"

We took the train for Leningrad that night. The railway station was clean and hot, crowded with people and the big statue of Lenin. The conductor of the Red Arrow train was a pretty girl, rather stout. The sleeping-compartment was comfortable and big. Alas, not big enough, though for both of us.

I explained to the conductor that in England it was just not done to put men and women in the same sleeper unless married.

"Ha ha, ho ho," laughed this stout little body, holding her sides.

People started to climb from the platform into the train to see the fun. "Ho, ho," they all roared. "Divorce! Scandal! Aren't the English a scream?"

Emmwood, who was drooping a bit with embarrassment, said not to pile it on. However, with some ceremony we were shown to separate sleepers at opposite ends of the coach.

Emmwood wanted to tip the conductor for our night's bottles of mineral water and glasses of tea. Tips were forbidden, but were sometimes gratefully received. So he handed over a 10-rouble note and the girl asked sweetly how much change we would like to have back. When he said "Nichevo" (nothing) she said, "I like the English tourists best. I go to evening classes to learn English. I can say 'Door', 'Window' and 'At what time do you like to stand up in the morning?'"

"You know," said Emmwood as we drove to our hotel, "I get the impression that these people are not as simple as they look."

We returned exhausted to London. "I've got a lovely trip coming up for you, you lucky girl," said features editor Marius Pope. "A whole fortnight just swanning round the coast of Spain and Portugal for a wine-tasting spree."

The trouble was I'd had enough free vodka and Georgian wines to last me for a bit. I wanted to go home, clean the flat, which needed it, do some shopping, just sleep. Even on a "jolly" I knew I still had to hunt around for stories and features.

I said I was all worn out, and why didn't he send Eve Perrick or someone else? My trouble was that my voice always took a nasty high note at times like these. Once, on a Moscow visit, I received a cable from the *Daily Sketch* boss, Walter Hayes, asking me to try and get an invitation for the Queen to go to Russia, and the pretty Moscow waitress in the white frilled cap who woke me up at 3 a.m. to hand me the cable said Boje moy (which means my God), she never knew an Englishwoman could be so passionate and say such awful things. And once at Rangoon airport I got a cable from Mr Pope telling me to get off whatever plane I was on and telephone the story about Suzy Wong, which I'd just been doing on a visit to the alleged brothel at Kowloon— a rather brown, miserable place which looked like a down-at-heel pub in Jarrow or Walsall—and the Indian gentleman who bought me a lemonade while I read the cable in the Rangoon airport canteen said "Oh dear, oh dear, lady, do try to calm yourself".

There could be no excuse. I had been a nice woman once. Now I wasn't. The reporting business, as I have pointed out in this little book, could change a woman's disposition, often, for the worse.

The features editor sent our Home Page girl, a nice, rather sad-looking blonde named Joy Matthews, on the wine-tasting "jolly". Three weeks later someone said "Did you hear about Joy? She's getting married!"

There had been twenty-eight people on that charter plane, including travel agents and businessmen in the wine trade. Joy was the only woman. At the head of the party was a young, attractive widower who was a director of the famous Bristol sherry firm.

Our then editor, William Hardcastle, said: "We are not losing a reporter so much as gaining a case of sherry."

But Mr Pope said to me, "It might have been you. You could have been the bride. Serves you right, old girl. Teach you not to be so nasty."

Well, it made me think. And I shuddered to think what Lily and Cousin Roz would say, when they heard.

CHAPTER XXXI

NO SEAT IN THE STREET

THE TROUBLE WITH having arrived, so to speak, in Fleet Street was that there was not, and probably never would be, any place to sit down. And after more than twenty-five years of the Street I felt like a sit-down. There were no editorial chairs in journalism for women, except on a few magazines which, however, was a different kind of business altogether.

Men could become editors, assistant editors or sub-editors or production editors or rewrite men or copy-tasters, which was the name given to the retired reporters who sat near the news editor in the news room and "tasted" the news as it came in, or sniffed at it with that long nose for news which they'd got to have, according to that Reuter man who first taught me the business. The important thing was that all these jobs were sitting-down jobs. Me—I was still on the road, or rather footing it up the Street, and, still overweight in spite of all the diets they put me on, it took me twice as long to get from Blackfriars up to that nice little tea-place near the Law Courts.

Of course, the business had changed enormously since I started. Girls nowadays didn't get the chance to see the world at the office expense, as I had done. Everyone had to specialise, too, even the news men, even the chaps who specialised in pop. Now there had to be a specialist doing telly-pop, and another one doing pop-news or any other kind of pop.

You could say I became a specialist too. No, not in the clowning business any more. That caught on so well that everyone started to get into the act, including my own colleague Boofy Gore (Lord Arran), and, on the other rival papers, every scarecrow of a

man weighing eight stone of skin and bone slimmed at a
clinic, or did an exercise stunt, or something. All the things done
on television now were done by us years before. The trouble was,
as I long ago found out, there just weren't any new stunts. The
main difference was that in our day we had to get the job done and
turn in the copy in twenty-four hours, and get on with the next
story. Nowadays a staff man got a week or even longer . . . no
wonder newspapers were no longer an economic proposition.
(But that's another story.)

No, I was still the specialist at . . . the-news editor-says-there's-
a-funny-man-downstairs-in-the-hall-can't-speak-English . . . sort
of thing. The stranger might be an Arab or a Portuguese or a
Congolese, say with just a little Dutch and nothing else. "Send
Olga," they always shouted. "Put Olga on it."

That was because of my name. And because Englishmen still
believed that all foreigners spoke the same funny language, an
un-English one, poor devils. The consolation was that if I'd
used my real name of Olga Izvozchik . . . well, I'd probably never
have "made" the Street at all. You couldn't have a name like
that in a by-line.

Meanwhile, things were changing for us. True, business got
much worse, but we felt that quite soon it was going to get better.
Newspapers had to keep changing, to keep alive. For a time
wonder drugs were out, and Bernard Levin and some intellectual
ideas were in. My stunts were reduced to a few per year. People
were tired of diets which never seemed to work for long. I was
sent on sporting stints instead, cycling, learning to ski, fishing,
running in Regent's Park with our political cartoonist, Leslie
Illingworth.

The cycling stint made quite a hit. I did fifty miles, with a
doctor (who trained Olympic champions) and Peter Haigh, up
and down the hills of Hertfordshire. The doctor brought supplies
of yoghourt and, as he cycled alongside, he kept egging me on:

"Stay on the saddle; don't get off; you can do it . . . you can . . . good girl . . . don't get OFF, you'll spoil the rhythm, marvellous, superb." It was all rather super, really. I wore special short-legged, corduroy knickers for this job, and I remember how they were handed round our office, from man to man, for everyone to see.

Bernard Levin, who is a rather conventional, terribly polite man, groaned and said, "If your poor Buba could see you now..."

My Buba, my Grandmother! My Babushka!

Yes, Grandma Izvozchik . . . she started me off, but Levin was right, she never would have liked Fleet Street or the knickers or anything . . .

Life, as I said, always gives you, in the end, what you want. Bettina, my youngest sister, had three sons, and the youngest of her twins, Bernard, is pure Izzy Izvozchik all over again. Bernard is now ten years old. "Ogg," he says to me, "Ogg, listen, you must listen. I've got a story for you." It's like having Father back again.

So the time is come to tell the ending which came also to my other characters.

Dr Margolin, for example, joined the British Army at the start of the war, was promoted to captain, and died of leukaemia after the war's end.

All my friends and relations in Poland and Russia were killed by the Germans. Except for Rudolf and his family, who escaped one day from Vichy France and took a boat from Marseilles to America. Rudolf and Anna ran a chicken farm in Los Angeles. Their daughter Ruth married and taught French at Philadelphia high school. The boy, my nephew Marcel Frenkel, became a professor of eye surgery at Chicago University.

The widows of Herr Süss and Herr Friedmann also live in Los Angeles now. Herr Doktor Mayer is retired and lives near London. Little Josie Berlinger has his own business near Mincing Lane. He found a wife in the end, and begat children. Now he is dead.

The general manager of Reuters, W. A. Cole, who first gave me my chance, died at fifty, for Fleet Street is a killer if you stick at it. Arthur Wilson, news editor in Newcastle, is gone too.

Roz and Rita and Hans May are dead. Lily still enjoys a happy married life.

As for me, my friend J is coming back to me for good, coming home after sixteen years, which is more, much more happiness than I deserve.

Aunt Becky and her family became the pride of the kibbutz at Mishmar Haemek, Israel.

Aunt Sally, last surviving member of the family of Izvozchiks from Utyena and Minsk, still lives in her little flat in St John's Wood, is rather silent and proud, and keeps herself to herself. She will not like this book at all. What can I do? Father always said I must write it if he never got around to doing it himself. And I do feel it might give the second and third generation of our lot something to have a row about. There's been nothing doing on those lines for ages.